What F

Ready, Set, Married

"Instructive, practical, and Biblically sound...Dr. Mendez calls us all to the 'high road' of a marriage grounded in God's Word and built up by the power of the Holy Spirit.
Kim Paul Storm, Ph.D.,
Clinical Psychologist and co-author of
Boxes of Secrets: Workbook/Devotional

Every engaged and married person ought to read and study this book. It is jam packed with Scriptural principles and relevant research on how to build a strong and lasting marriage. Dr. Mendez's rich counseling experience makes this book invaluable in helping couples understand the essential components of a happy marriage. I plan on giving it to every couple I marry so that they might experience the joy of marriage as God intended.

Roger Sonnenberg, Senior Pastor,
Our Savior Lutheran Church,
Author of *501 Practical Ways to Love Your Wife and Kids*

Ready, Set, Married

12 Christian Character Traits for a Strong and Lasting Marriage

Buddy Mendez, Ph.D.

Copyright © 2011 by Buddy Mendez, Ph.D.

All rights reserved. No part of this book may be used, reproduced, stored in a retrieval system, or transmitted in any form whatsoever — including electronic, photocopy, recording — without prior written permission from the author, except in the case of brief quotations embodied in critical articles or reviews.

Scripture quotations are taken from the *Holy Bible, New International Version®*. *NIV®*. Copyright © 1973, 1978, 1984 by International Bible Society. Used by permission of Zondervan. All rights reserved.

FIRST EDITION

ISBN: 9781936989232

Library of Congress Control Number: 2011938032

Published by

P.O. Box 2839, Apopka, FL 32704

Printed in the United States of America

Disclaimer: The views and opinions expressed in this book are solely those of the authors and other contributors. These views and opinions do not necessarily represent those of Certa Resources LLC, dba Certa Publishing.

Dedication

*To Aaron, Brennon, Malia and Blake.
May your marriages be blessed by the
power and love of Christ.*

Table of Contents

Introduction 9
1. Commitment 13
2. Honesty 21
3. Unselfishness 29
4. Humility 37
5. Forgiveness 47
6. Empathy 57
7. Respect 67
8. Intimacy 77
9. Patience 87
10. Kindness 93
11. Peace 103
12. Maturity 119
References 131
Acknowledgements 135
About The Author 136

Introduction

One of the most frequent questions I get in my line of work is, "How can I make my marriage last?" This book is an attempt to answer that question. The insights and principles I present in this book emanate from my study of God's world (scientific research) and God's Word (Scripture). My hope is that these Christian principles will guide couples toward greater security and satisfaction in their marriages.

Each chapter in this book starts with Scripture that espouses a particular Christian character trait. The body of the chapter defines and describes how to apply that trait from both a Biblical and psychological perspective. At the end of each chapter, I have included questions designed to stimulate further discussion. Lastly, I prescribe a weekly challenge to encourage readers to apply what they have learned to their romantic relationship.

Although I often talk about marriage in the following pages, this book can be helpful to all couples, whether they are married, engaged or even just beginning to date. I have set out to write a short, straightforward and practical book based on my experience as a counselor, teacher and student of marriage. I have tried to distill my thoughts on how to build and maintain a strong marriage into the following twelve chapters.

Before you begin reading this book, I want to emphasize that it promotes the *pursuit* of ideals for marriage, not the *mastery* of ideals. No one can perfectly do what I suggest in the following chapters. God understands this. The Bible clearly teaches that although Christians are saved from the penalty of sin by the blood of Christ, we still can expect to fall short of God's standards for holiness this side of the grave.

Therefore, I urge you to approach this book with humility. Remember that you will never become a perfect husband or wife. On the other hand, it is crucial to know that when we inevitably fail, God still loves us, forgives us and encourages us to press on. Satan wants us to believe that since we cannot be perfect, we should not even try to honor God with our romantic relationships.

I believe God is not only honored but also pleased when we try. He has given us guidelines for living in this world to protect us from the pain and anguish of a broken relationship. In addition, I believe that God will help us put these Biblical principles into practice. Paul says, "I can do all things through Him who gives me strength." (Philippians 4:13) We are not alone in this journey. We have been given the Holy Spirit to prompt us, encourage us and strengthen us when we feel weak, weary and heavy-laden (Matthew 11:28).

It is my hope that you will not use this book as a means of demeaning or criticizing your partner. Instead, think about how these principles can lead to positive changes in your own character that will create a climate favorable to positive change in your partner. In other words, try to avoid the temptation of pointing out the speck in your partner's eye when you may have a log in your own.

Finally, remember to "submit to one another out of reverence for Christ." (Ephesians 5:21) In other words, love your partner not because he or she loves you first, but rather because you love and respect the God of creation, who has chosen to love you without condition and in ways beyond your comprehension.

My hope and prayer is that God will richly bless you as you discover the wonders of His grace and love in loving union with your spouse.

~ Chapter 1 ~

Commitment

"Guard yourself in your spirit, and do not break faith with the wife of your youth." (Malachi 2:15b)

"What God has joined together let man not separate." (Matthew 19:6)

The simple teaching of the Bible is this, "Once married, always married." This perspective is quite different than the secular view of marriage that says, "I will stay married to you as long as I feel I am in love with you." The problem with the latter approach to marriage is that it is perfectly normal in the course of any marriage to not "feel" in love with your spouse. As an engaged couple, this may be hard to comprehend. However, if you ask any couple who has been married for longer than five years, they will tell you that feelings wax and wane throughout the course of marriage.

Therefore, the decision to remain in marriage should never be based on one's feelings. Instead, as Christians, we are called to choose to love our spouses in the same unconditional manner that Christ has chosen to love us. The Bible confirms the validity of this approach in 1 Corinthians 13:4-7, in which love is beautifully described as volitional as opposed to emotional:

> Love is patient, love is kind. It does not envy, it does not boast, it is not proud. It is not rude, it is not self-seeking, it is not easily angered, it keeps no record of wrongs. Love does not delight in evil but rejoices with the truth. It always protects, always trusts, always hopes, always perseveres.

Although feelings of love are enjoyable and desirable, they are not a necessary condition for love to exist. When feelings of love fade, couples need not panic. Rather, they should see these times as opportunities to extend love through actions until loving feelings inevitably return. This can only be done when couples make a commitment to love one another in spite of how they may feel at any particular moment and regardless of how their spouses respond to their gestures of love.

Contemporary research findings support the notion that couples who stay committed through the tough times can regain the happiness they once had. In a longitudinal study reported by The Institute for American Values, researchers found that of 645 unhappy spouses, two out of three who chose not to divorce or separate ended up happily married five years later (Waite, Browning, Doherty, Gallagher, Luo, & Stanley, 2002).

What is Christian Commitment?

From a Christian perspective there are three types of commitment that strengthen marriages: (1) Commitment to God, (2) Commitment to one's spouse and (3) Commitment to the welfare of the marriage.

Commitment To God

The first and most important commitment is to God. As Christians, our chief purpose is to glorify God with our lives. Romans 12:1-2 states:

> Therefore, I urge you, brothers, in view of God's mercy, to offer your bodies as living sacrifices, holy and pleasing to God—this is your spiritual act of worship. Do not conform any longer to the pattern of this world, but be transformed by the renewing of your mind. Then you will be able to test and approve God's good, pleasing and perfect will.

Ephesians 5:17-20 offers further guidance on God's will:

> Therefore do not be foolish, but understand what the Lord's will is. Do not get drunk on wine, which leads to debauchery. Instead be filled with the Spirit. Speak to one another with psalms, hymns and spiritual songs. Sing and make music in your heart to the Lord, always giving thanks to God the Father for everything, in the name of our Lord Jesus Christ.

Our commitment to God is a decision to be filled with the Holy Spirit, as we confess our sins, receive His grace and are empowered to bear the fruits of the spirit outlined in Galatians 5:22: "But the fruit of the Spirit is love, joy, peace, patience, kindness, goodness, faithfulness, gentleness, and self-control."

Commitment To Our Spouses

Our second commitment is to our spouses. Ephesians 5:21-27 gives us guidance regarding our commitment to each other:

> Submit to one another, out of reverence for Christ. Wives, submit to your husbands as to the Lord. For the husband is the head of the wife as Christ is the head of the church, his body, of which he is the Savior. Now as the church submits to Christ, so also wives should submit to their husbands in everything. Husbands, love your wives, just as Christ loved the church and gave himself up for her to make her holy, cleansing her by the washing with water through the word, and to present her to himself as a radiant church, without stain or wrinkle or any other blemish, but holy and blameless.

It is important to note that this passage does not support or encourage men to dominate or exert unfair control over their wives. In Ephesians 5:21 each spouse is encouraged to "submit to one another." Christ loved the Church through humility, sacrifice and service. Thus, husbands ought to exercise their leadership in the home in the same manner. This passage can be summarized by another passage, from Galatians 5:13: "Do not use your freedom to indulge the sinful nature; rather serve one another in love." Our commitment to serving each other is never easy due to our sinful and selfish nature. It is not the first thing that will come to our minds, but it is the best way to maintain a loving relationship.

Commitment To The Marriage

Our third commitment is to the marriage. This type of commitment is described as "personal dedication" by authors, Stanley, Trathen, McCain and Bryan (1998) in their book, *A Lasting Promise: A Christian Guide to Fighting for Your Marriage*. According to these authors, personal dedication is comprised of the following five characteristics:

Desiring the long-term: This refers to a couple's wish for the relationship to work out over the long term. As my former professor, Dr. Richard Hunt, once told me, "There is no escape hatch in a Christian marriage." In other words, when Christian couples encounter problems, they don't contemplate leaving, but rather focus on finding solutions and making necessary behavioral changes. Husbands and wives who refuse to leave when the going gets tough are rewarded with character growth.

The priority of the relationship: The relationship is given top priority over work, children, parents, money and even ministry. One of the things I am constantly battling in my work with couples is their tendency to attend to other matters of life before they attend to their marriage. The most common dynamics I see are husbands prioritizing work over marriage and wives prioritizing children over husbands. Often, couples are just too tired to interact with each other in any meaningful way because they have expended their energy attending to less important matters throughout the day. By the time these couples are ready to focus on each other, all they can think about is sleep.

We-ness: This refers to the degree to which each spouse views their relationship as two individuals working together for the sake of one team. In my private practice, I often exhort couples to come to a "we" decision rather than settle for a "you" or an "I" decision. This helps them to resolve conflicts and solve problems. It also leads to a sense of equal participation and fairness in the relationship. Arriving at a "we" decision or solution requires relinquishing one's personal freedom. Each spouse can no longer choose to live life on his or her own terms. I often gently remind couples that the decision to marry is also a decision to give up a degree of personal autonomy. However, I also remind them that the joys of "oneness" far outweigh the costs. Psychological research supports the benefits of "*we-ness*." Studies have shown that satisfied couples enjoy working together as a team because they realize that what is good for the team is ultimately best for them as individuals (Stanley, et al., 1998).

Satisfaction with sacrifice: This refers to our willingness to extend personal resources such as time, energy and effort for the sake of the relationship. I often share with couples that marriages are like fruit trees; they need to be nourished and cared for in order to mature and produce good fruit. If a fruit tree is left alone it will slowly wither, produce less fruit each successive season and eventually die. Couples benefit from making the sacrifices that are necessary to give their relationship the water, sunlight, warmth and rich soil it needs to produce a bountiful harvest.

Alternative monitoring: This pertains to our ability to resist serious consideration of alternative partners. This may involve excessive flirting, indulging in mental fantasies with other people or even pushing the limits of a platonic friendship. Jesus warns us to resist these temptations. He says, "You have heard that it was said, 'do not commit adultery.' But I tell you that anyone who looks at a woman lustfully has already committed adultery with her in his heart." (Matthew 5:27, 28) There is nothing more damaging to a relationship than infidelity, regardless of whether it exists in our behavior or in our hearts. I have seen too many marriages devastated by the consequences of infidelity. The rupture of trust in these cases is a deep and, in some cases, fatal wound to the marriage.

The good news is that Jesus can help us resist the temptations that the enemy inevitably throws our way. The word of God tells us that God's peace can "guard our hearts and our minds in Christ Jesus." (Philippians 4:7) God wants to protect us from the deceptive schemes of the devil. Paul reminds us in his letter to the Corinthians that "No temptation has seized you except what is common to man. And God is faithful; he will not let you be tempted beyond what you can bear. But when you are tempted, he will also provide a way out so that you can stand up under it." (1 Corinthians 10:13) We must rely on the Holy Spirit to guide us away from temptations and toward His plan and purpose for our marriage.

Questions for Reflection:

1. What type of commitment was demonstrated to you by your parents? What would you like to change and what would you like to retain in your own marriage?

2. What is the water, sunlight, rich soil and warmth that you think your relationship needs in order to grow and produce good fruit?

3. As you look at the various aspects of "personal dedication" proposed by Stanley, et al., which of these will be the most difficult for you to put into practice? Why?

Weekly Challenge:

Make one sacrifice for the sake of your relationship each day this week. At the end of each day, discuss with your partner how your daily sacrifice affected your relationship.

~ Chapter 2 ~

Honesty

"Surely you desire truth in the inner parts." (Psalm 51:6a)

"Love does not delight in evil but rejoices with the truth." (1 Corinthians 13:6)

"Therefore each of you must put off falsehood and speak truthfully to his neighbor for we are all members of one body." (Ephesians 4:25)

The research on truthfulness in relationships is alarming. In one study of university students, 92% of the participants admitted to having lied to a romantic partner (Knox, Schacht, Holt, & Turner, 1993). In addition, researchers have found that romantic partners tend to have a difficult time detecting deception and tend to assume that their partners are being truthful (Levine & McCornack, 1992; Stiff, Kim, & Ramesh, 1992). These findings are very troubling especially given other research which has found that when a lie is discovered by a romantic partner, significant negative emotional reactions are likely to occur in the relationship (McCornack & Levine, 1990).

The Bible teaches that honesty is an important aspect of healthy relationships. Scripture tells us that honesty is like a kiss on the lips (Proverbs 24:26), and Paul reminds us to put off falsehood and speak truthfully to our neighbors (Ephesians 4:25). Like a kiss, honesty leads to feelings of warmth, closeness and connection. Without honesty it is very difficult to build trust or to express vulnerability. Without trust and vulnerability, our heartfelt longings for deep connections are short-circuited.

Despite the teaching of the Bible and the ample research evidence supporting the timeless truth that "honesty is the best policy," many spouses continue to deceive one another. Why does this still happen? The short answer is that even though we are viewed as saints through the blood of Christ, we still live imperfect lives this side of the grave. The longer answer takes into account the various psychological and spiritual factors that make dishonesty hard to resist.

From a Christian perspective, lying is as old as Adam and Eve. The Bible tells us that before sin entered the world, Adam and Eve were "naked and not ashamed." (Genesis 2:25) While they were in this state, there was no reason to lie because they were sinless and therefore not ashamed of themselves. After they disobeyed God and sin entered the world, things changed. With sin, came shame. Adam and Eve no longer felt comfortable in their physical, psychological and spiritual nakedness. They attempted to hide their shame by covering themselves with fig leaves.

In our marriages, we often act like Adam and Eve. In our attempts to ward off feelings of shame, we hide behind a lie. We do not share with our spouses the areas of our lives in which we feel shame. We hide when we fear we have disappointed our spouses or have not lived up to our perception of his or her standards for us. We try to make ourselves look like what we expect ourselves to be. We embellish and exaggerate the positives, while ignoring and discounting the negative aspects of our character and behavior.

We hide behind lies because we anticipate that, at best, our partners will disapprove of our true self, and, at worst, may even stop loving us when they discover who we really are. We fear rejection and abandonment, so we live inauthentic lives, seeking to impress and please, rather than pursuing honest transparency. The trouble with this lifestyle is that it prevents the "oneness" that God desires in marriage.

Another problem with deceit is that when we hide behind a façade, we cannot feel truly loved because we do not feel truly known. We see our spouses loving our persona rather than our person. This leads to feelings of detachment and aloneness. This is not God's intent. Before sin entered the world, God said, "It is not good for the man to be alone. I will make a helper suitable for him." (Genesis 2:18) Furthermore, Genesis 2:24 demonstrates God's desire for a husband and a wife: "For this reason a man will leave his father and mother and be united to his wife, and they will become one flesh." God wants us to be intimately unified to one another in truth, not deceptively disconnected by falsehood.

Coming Out Of Hiding

What can we do to resist the temptation to perpetuate falsehood? First, we need to realize that God knows us better than we know ourselves and yet still chooses to love us. The Bible says, "God demonstrates his own love for us in this: While we were still sinners, Christ died for us." (Romans 5:8) Although we are imperfect and flawed, God still finds us to be so valuable that He sacrificed His Son for our sake. If we can seek our worth in God rather than through the things of this world (money, power, prestige, fame, beauty, knowledge, possessions, athleticism, etc.), then we can be comfortable sharing our true selves with our spouses. When we do this, our spouse has the opportunity to love us as God loves him or her; unconditionally, faithfully and passionately. As we experience this love, we feel less shame and more of the oneness we crave. This encourages us to continue to live in truth. As my former professor John Finch once told me, "God has given us a creative directive to be ourselves in truth relentlessly." God has created us to function optimally when we live in truth in our marriages.

There is a second common reason we do not speak truthfully to each other. We are afraid to engage in conflict. Conflict avoiders fear that if they embrace problems head on, their relationship will inevitably suffer devastating consequences. This fear may be based on previous relational experiences where the expression of conflict has been associated with negative experiences such as anger, resentment, criticism, defensiveness and possibly even violence. Thus, the conflict avoiders prefer to suppress their complaints, not ask for what they want and subordinate their own needs to the needs of their partner. This can lead to feelings of resentment, depression, anxiety and psychosomatic symptoms such as headaches, physical aches and pain and loss of energy. It can also lead to what psychologists call "passive-aggressive" behavior.

Passive-Aggressive Behavior

What is Passive-aggressive behavior? I define it as any act or failure to act that allows the conflict avoider to express unconscious aggressive impulses in a disguised manner. Passive-aggressive acts help the conflict avoider consciously believe they are not generating or escalating conflict while simultaneously allowing them the satisfaction of "punishing" his or her spouse when he or she feels wronged. It is important to note that passive-aggressive behavior is almost always unconscious. The perpetrators often have no idea what they are doing to hurt their spouses, because they have repressed their own feelings of hurt, pain and anger.

For example, a wife who is afraid to tell her husband that she resents having to schedule his medical appointments may "forget" to schedule an important appointment. This example illustrates that passive-aggressive behavior works and yet doesn't work. It works in the sense that the wife has avoided a conflict over who should schedule appointments. However, it doesn't work in the sense that the husband will likely be upset with his wife for forgetting. He might say something harsh such as, "How can you possibly forget something so important? Don't you care about my health?" His wife would then probably feel hurt and unjustly attacked. However, since she prefers to avoid conflict with her husband, she will not express these feelings. Instead she might say something like, "I'm sorry honey, I'll try and remember to do it tomorrow," and then change the subject. The cycle is completed when her unacknowledged hurt and anger pull her toward further passive-aggressive behavior such as "accidentally" overcooking her husband's dinner that night.

How can someone overcome passive-aggressive behavior? The first step is to ask yourself if you might feel angry when you feel hurt or sad. The second step is to express your complaints clearly and in love rather than holding them inside. Chapter 11 will describe appropriate ways to resolve conflict in more detail.

Questions for Reflection:

1. What keeps you from being completely honest with your partner?

2. What parts of yourself do you attempt to hide from your partner?

3. What types of conflicts do you tend to avoid? What are you afraid will happen if you try to make peace rather than keep peace?

Weekly Challenge:

Tell your spouse something this week that you have previously kept hidden. It doesn't have to be a deep dark secret, just something you haven't mentioned because you were afraid of how it would make you look.

~ Chapter 3 ~

Unselfishness

"Turn my heart toward your statutes and not toward selfish gain." (Psalm 119:36)

"Do nothing out of selfish ambition or vain conceit, but in humility consider others better than yourselves. Each of you should look not only to your own interests, but also to the interests of others." (Philippians 2:3,4)

"Love is not self-seeking." (1 Corinthians 13:5)

Most popular psychology and self-help books these days are titled something along the lines of, "Ten easy ways to manipulate the one you love so they can meet your selfish needs." In fact, many people today spend thousands of dollars on therapy and workshops to become more adept at getting their "needs met." Sadly, these people are not really learning about healthy self-care. Rather, they are learning how to indulge and gratify their sinful nature. Unfortunately, many well-meaning counselors teach that the Biblical call to care for others before oneself is some type of co-dependent psychopathology.

As Christians, we need to stand on the truth of Scripture, rather than the so-called wisdom of professionals who align their practices with the prevailing trends of contemporary society. We need to take seriously God's command to love our spouses sacrificially. Psychiatrist, Scott Peck, has offered a definition of love that approximates the unselfish nature of Biblical love in his classic book, *The Road Less Traveled* (1978). He has written: "I define love thus: The will to extend one's self for the purpose of nurturing one's own or another's spiritual growth (Peck, 1978 p. 81)." I believe this definition is useful but incomplete. I prefer to define Christian love as, "The will to extend oneself for the purpose of advancing another's physical, psychological, emotional and spiritual growth and well-being." In other words, loving another means helping them to become all that God has created them to be in mind, body and spirit.

Living and loving unselfishly is difficult. When we feel hurt or neglected, our sinful nature tells us to control our spouse for the sake of our own agenda through the invocation of guilt, shame or fear. This strategy ends up damaging our relationship even more as our spouse typically reacts to feeling attacked, and thus fortifies his or her own defenses at best, and at worst, he or she responds with counterattacks. Our response to defensiveness or counterattacks is then to attack and defend more rigorously. This response further entangles couples in a seemingly endless spiral of conflict.

Finding A Way Out Of Selfishness

Fortunately, God provides a way out. The Bible implores us to seek God's ways rather than our own. Proverbs 3:5, 6 states, "Trust in the Lord with all your heart and lean not on your own understanding, in all your ways acknowledge Him and He will make your paths straight." The Biblical path is simple and yet extremely difficult. We must always seek first the well-being and interests of our spouse. We need to reflect on the question, "How can I care for my spouse, encourage his or her faith and enrich his or her life?" Next, we need to take our answers and put them into practice, as we make specific behavioral changes through the empowerment of the Holy Spirit.

In his commentary on First Corinthians, Gordon Fee speaks of unselfish love in the following manner:

> It does not seek its own; it does not believe that "finding oneself" is the highest good; it is not enamored with self-gain, self-justification, self-worth. To the contrary, it seeks the good of one's neighbor—or enemy (Fee, 1987).

Paul describes our Christian duty to follow after Christ's example of unselfish love in the book of Romans:

> We who are strong ought to bear with the failings of the weak and not to please ourselves. Each of us should please his neighbor for his good, to build him

up. For even Christ did not please himself but as it is written, "The insults of those who insult you have fallen on me." (Romans 15:1-3)

A beautiful thing occurs when each spouse behaves unselfishly for the sake of Christ. A new pattern is established. Unselfish love elicits responses of gentleness and compassion rather than defensiveness, criticism or withdrawal. The unselfish couple enjoys a positive spiral of mutual unselfishness and reciprocal kindness. This new pattern continues as long as each partner continues to maintain an outward focus. As the Bible says, "Seek first his kingdom and his righteousness, and all these things will be given to you as well." (Matthew 6:33)

Research On Unselfishness

The Biblical principle of unselfishness has received little attention in the psychological research literature, but what little research we have supports its usefulness in relationships of all kinds.

For instance, psychologist, Dr. Bernard Rimland (1982) has investigated the relationship between selfishness and happiness in a study of 216 college students. These students were asked to write the names of up to 10 persons whom they knew best, and after each name, the students were to designate whether each person was happy or unhappy and selfish or unselfish. The results provided remarkable support for the notion that unselfishness leads to happiness. Only 78 people whom the students rated as selfish were also rated as happy, while 827 people whom the students rated as unselfish were also rated as happy.

In a more recent study, Sappington (1998) studied the relationship between selfishness and anger related problems for 186 college students at the University of Alabama. The results of his study found that the unselfish students were significantly less likely to experience anger related problems in their relationships with others.

What Unselfishness Is Not

It is important to note that living unselfishly does not mean that Christians ought to become doormats. There are times when we must stand up for our own rights in a loving manner.

Dr. Lewis Smedes has identified three instances when our own needs rightfully need to be asserted in his book, *Love Within Limits* (1978). First of all, we should assert our needs when our neighbor can be helped. For example, if a wife has a need for her husband to pay close attention to her when she talks about issues that are important to her, she should ask her husband to listen carefully when she speaks, because it will help her husband grow in compassion, empathy and humility. Disciplining himself to pay close attention to her will likely result in him paying careful attention to the important issues of others, such as his children, friends, family and co-workers, who will in turn also benefit.

A second instance occurs when it is necessary to seek one's

needs in order to pursue one's calling as a member of the body of Christ. God has created us for a purpose. Jesus has given us the great commission to "go and make disciples of all nations." (Matthew 28:19,20) Paul reminds believers that, "Each one should retain the place in life that the Lord assigned to him and to which God has called him." (1 Corinthians 7:17a) Paul also states, "We know that in all things God works for the good of those who love him, who have been called according to his purpose." (Romans 8:28) God has placed a divine call on each of us whom He has saved (Romans 8:30), and it is His will that we do what is necessary to fulfill that call. As Smedes (1987, p.41) has so simply and accurately written, "I must demand my rights so that I can take care of my corner of God's earth."

The third occasion in which it is necessary to assert our needs occurs when we are not treated with the value God intends. Smedes has stated, "We have an undeniable right to be what we truly are and to be known as what we are" (Smedes, 1987, p.41). It is true that we are sinners who have no inherent value apart from Christ. However, in Christ, we are also image bearers who have been cleansed of all unrighteousness and reconciled to our Father. As children of God, who have been redeemed by the creator of the universe, we must protect our right to be treated with respect and dignity in our marriages. Scripture tells us to "show proper respect to everyone" (1 Peter 2:17) and to "submit to one another." (Ephesians 5:21)

Questions for Reflection:

1. How have you behaved selfishly in your relationship? Give specific examples.

2. How can your partner advance your physical, psychological, emotional and spiritual growth?

3. What needs should you assert in order to protect your dignity, pursue your calling and love your neighbor?

Weekly Challenge:

During this next week, perform an unselfish act of service for your partner. At the end of the week see if he or she can guess what it was.

~ Chapter 4 ~

Humility

"This is the one I esteem: he who is humble and contrite in spirit, and trembles at my word." (Isaiah 66:2b)

"The fear of the Lord teaches a man wisdom, and humility comes before honor." (Proverbs 15:33)

"Humble yourselves before the Lord, and he will lift you up." (James 4:10)

"He has showed you, O man, what is good. And what does the Lord require of you? To act justly, and to love mercy and to walk humbly with your God." (Micah 6:8)

Most Christians would agree that marriages benefit when spouses display an attitude of humility. Asking Christians to define humility, however, might not result in such a consensus. Fortunately, the Bible gives us a description of true humility we can all agree upon. Paul's exhortation to the Church at Rome provides ample guidance. Paul has written,

"For by the grace given me I say to every one of you: Do not think of yourself more highly than you ought, but rather think of yourself with sober judgment, in accordance with the measure of faith God has given you." (Romans 12:3) This passage tells us that true humility is rooted in an accurate and truthful estimation of oneself.

Psychologists agree with this view of humility. For example, Emmons (2000) has nicely distinguished humility from self-denigration:

> To be humble is not to have a low opinion of oneself; it is to have an opinion of oneself that is no better or worse than the opinion one holds of others. It is the ability to keep one's talents and accomplishments in perspective...to have a sense of self-acceptance, an understanding of one's imperfections, and to be free from arrogance and low self-esteem." (pp. 164-165)

Sadly, our sinful nature makes it difficult to form an accurate opinion of ourselves. As a result, a common goal of psychotherapy is to help clients develop more realistic self-appraisals. For instance, children who are criticized, dismissed and devalued will likely develop into adults with negative self-perceptions. These distortions are usually expressed in one of two ways. On the one hand, a person may berate themselves verbally and behave in a self-effacing manner. This pattern has often been referred to as "false humility." On the other hand, a person might repress their self-critical beliefs in order to ward off painful feelings of shame and worthlessness. This adaptation usually leads to the development of a "grandiose self" characterized by conceit, arrogance and extreme sensitivity to criticism. Clinical psychologists refer to this as a narcissistic style. As Christians we think of it as false pride. Either adaptation is detrimental to marriages.

Sin not only affects our self-perception, it also affects how others perceive us and how we perceive how others perceive us. This is a critical problem since our self-concept is profoundly influenced by what we believe to be the collective appraisals of significant others. An illustration of how a person can misperceive another can be found by looking at a defensive process known as projection. Projection occurs when a person sees in others their own shortcomings in order to ward off feelings of personal shame. Jesus spoke of this phenomenon when He said, "Why do you look at the speck of sawdust in your brother's eye and pay no attention to the plank in your own eye?" (Matthew 7:4) Jesus is addressing the issue of inaccurately seeing in others what we fail to see in ourselves. I see this problem often in my private practice. I encourage spouses to ask themselves if they possess the very character flaw that they are seeing in their spouse.

The important question is this: How can we formulate an accurate self-appraisal in spite of our own depravity? The answer is that we can't. Only with the help of God can we truly know who we are. God has revealed our true nature in Scripture. As Martin Luther has stated, the Bible portrays us as simultaneously saints and sinners. Let's look at each of these aspects of our new nature as Christians.

We Are Sinners

The fallen nature of all humans, including the children of Israel, is clearly evident from the earliest of times. Abraham's lying about Sarah, Samson's failure to resist temptation and David's selfish desires for another man's wife are just a few examples. The Bible tells us we are imperfect sinners who deserve nothing, and can do nothing of real value apart from God. John 15:5b reads, "I am the vine; you are the branches. If a man remains in me and I in him, he will bear much fruit; apart from me you can do nothing." 1 John 1:10 says, "If we claim we have not sinned, we make him out to be a liar and his word has no place in our lives." The prophet Jeremiah has written, "The heart is deceitful above all things and beyond cure. Who can understand it?" (Jeremiah 17:9)

Even our so-called righteous acts are too often rooted in selfish motives. We pretend to be altruistic when we are really searching for social status and recognition in our community. The prophet Isaiah has proclaimed, "All of us have become like one who is unclean, and all our righteous acts are like filthy rags; we all shrivel up like a leaf and like the wind our sins sweep us away." (Isaiah 64:6) Scripture has made it abundantly clear that even as Christians, we are capable of making mistakes, hurting others and disobeying God. Humility demands that we admit and confess that we are sinners.

The good news is that when we acknowledge the reality of our own sinfulness, God can transform us by His grace.

Martin Luther once said, "When a man believes himself to be utterly lost light breaks." The Bible clearly teaches that when we go to God in humility and honesty He will save us. John writes, "If we confess our sins, he is faithful and just and will forgive us our sins and purify us from all unrighteousness." (1 John 1:9) Paul has written, "But God demonstrates his own love for us in this: While we were sinners, Christ died for us." (Romans 5:8) Paul also taught, "For it is by grace you have been saved, through faith—and this not from yourselves, it is the gift of God—not by works, so that no one can boast." (Ephesians 2:8-9) The above passages show us that forgiveness and salvation are not earned through good works; rather, they are freely given by God because He loves us. In other words, there is no sin greater than God's forgiveness.

The practical implications of forgiveness in marriage are profound. We are free to admit our mistakes, acknowledge our shortcomings and seek forgiveness from our spouse on a continual basis. We are free to speak to our spouse in phrases such as, "I'm sorry," "I was wrong" and "I made a mistake." This approach will benefit our marriages in several ways. One benefit is that our spouse will feel valued and respected. Everett Worthington, Jr. has noted this in his book, *Value Your Mate* (1993). He writes:

> True faith in Christ produces love. True love admits mistakes rather than defending them. To confess mistakes empowers one's partner. It says: "You are important to me. I am willing to humble my pride for you. I want you to stop hurting." Sincere confession is a way of loving, a way of valuing. (p. 64)

A second benefit occurs when, through confession, we short circuit the process of adding pain to the original wound. Worthington (1993) writes, "When we refuse to acknowledge our insensitivity or mistakes, our partner may interpret that as a lack of care—which often does more damage to a marriage than the original hurt (p. 64)." On the other hand, the book of James reminds us that healing comes with confession: "Therefore confess your sins to each other and pray for each other so that you may be healed." (James 5:16)

The following example illustrates the benefits of confession. Sharon promises her husband Rick that she will attend his basketball game, but she gets so caught up in her work that she loses track of time and arrives at half time. When Rick sees her walk in the gym late, he feels upset and wonders to himself if Sharon values her time at work more than time with him. Rick then ignores his wife when she says hello. At this point, Sharon gets defensive and says, "Give me a break. I had a lot of work to do. Stop acting like a child. It's not like you've never been late coming home." This increases Rick's frustration and anger. He yells back at her and they begin to fight.

But what if Sharon had apologized for being late? What if she had simply said, "I'm sorry Rick, I know how important it was for me to see the whole game. I blew it." This would be an honest admission of her mistake, regardless of whether it was intentional or not. Chances are Rick would respond with compassion and forgiveness. This would then lead to both Rick and Sharon having an enjoyable evening together.

We Are Saints

Happily, there is more to the story of who we are in Christ. The good news is that God has given the gift of the Holy Spirit to guide us in truth and empower us to do what is pleasing to God. Paul has written, "And he who searches our hearts knows the mind of the Spirit, because the Spirit intercedes for the saints in accordance with God's will." (Romans 8:27) In another related passage the author of Hebrews has written:

> May the God of peace, who through the blood of the eternal covenant brought back from the dead our Lord Jesus, that great Shepherd of the sheep, equip you with everything good for doing his will, and may he work in us what is pleasing to him, through Jesus Christ, to whom be glory forever and ever. Amen. (Hebrews 13:21, 22)

Fortunately, we do not need to succumb to the fatalistic view that we are doomed to fail God on a regular basis. Rather, we are free to pursue holiness, knowing that we will never be perfect. Martin Luther warned us against temptation to become lazy as Christians when he wrote, "the more certain we are about the freedom granted to us by Christ, the more unresponsive and slothful we are in presenting the Word, praying, doing good works, enduring evil, and the like (Gaebler, 2002)." The apostle Paul echoed the sentiments of Luther in his letter to the Philippians:

> Not that I have already obtained all this, or have already been made perfect but I press on to take hold of that

for which Christ Jesus took hold of me. Brothers, I do not consider myself yet to have taken hold of it. But one thing I do: Forgetting what is behind and straining toward what is ahead, I press on toward the goal to win the prize for which God has called me heavenward in Christ Jesus. (Philippians 3:12-14)

We should never say to our spouse, "I know I messed up again, but that's just the way I am." Rather, we are free to say, "I'm sorry I hurt you. I will pray that by the grace of God I can do better, and I will try to do better next time." The latter approach is much more in line with the Biblical principle of repentance. Theologians tell us that repentance means that, in addition to feeling remorse for our actions and confessing our sinfulness to God and one another, we also seek to do a 180-degree reversal in terms of our attitudes and behavior.

In summary, as saints, we can and should serve our spouse by making honest attempts to make the specific attitudinal and behavioral changes they desire which are pleasing to God. We must avoid the temptation to rationalize laziness and selfishness as inevitable consequences of our sinful nature. We need to say along with the Apostle Paul, "I can do everything through him who gives me strength." (Philippians 4:13)

Questions for Reflection:

1. What types of appraisals have you received from significant others growing up?

2. What makes it difficult for you to admit your mistakes to your partner?

3. What aspect of your character would you like to change? How are you going to try to do this?

Weekly Challenge:

Say each of the following sometime this week: I'm sorry. I was wrong. I made a mistake. Notice how you feel and how your partner responds. Discuss this with your partner.

~ Chapter 5 ~

Forgiveness

"Bear with each other and forgive whatever grievances you may have against one another. Forgive as the Lord forgave you." (Colossians 3:13).

"Do not take revenge, my friends, but leave room for God's wrath, for it is written: It is mine to avenge; I will repay, says the Lord." (Romans 12:19)

What Is forgiveness?

I define forgiveness as an intentional decision to do the following things: (1) to resist the urge to retaliate, (2) to no longer ruminate on the hurt and (3) to pray for the offender. Let's look more closely at these three components of forgiveness.

We Do Not Retaliate

First of all, those who forgive choose to not retaliate. The Bible tells us that we need to leave judgment and vengeance to God

(Romans 12:19). In marriage, we must remember that neither spouse is perfect. Hurting each other is inevitable. When we are hurt, it is much more effective to say, "Ouch," than to hurt back. My pastor once told me that, "Hurt people, hurt people." This is often the case. Nevertheless, in marriage it must be avoided. We need to honestly share with our spouses how and where they have hurt us. If we don't do this and instead yield to the sinful nature's desire for us to get even, our conflict will get worse and our relationship will suffer. The quickest way to avoid the escalation of conflict in your marriage is to immediately express your hurt rather than hurting back. Usually, you will find that underneath your feelings of anger toward your spouse will lay feelings of pain. Focus on the hurt, not the anger, and your relational wounds will be healed rather than deepened.

We Do Not Ruminate On The Hurt

Second, it is important to not think obsessively about the hurt. This does not mean that we do not allow ourselves to experience and express the feelings associated with the hurt. The expression of feelings is necessary and healthy. However, it is not healthy to intentionally and constantly focus our thoughts on the hurt. When we do this, we make it very difficult to move on with our lives, and resentment builds in our hearts. The Bible speaks to this point: "Do not conform any longer to the pattern of this world, but be transformed by the renewing of your mind." (Romans 12:2-3) The world tells us to resent those who mistreat us and to even the score. The Bible tells us to be like Christ, who forgave the sins of the world though the world despised Him. We are transformed when we stop looking back at the disappointments of our lives which cannot be changed, and focus on the future which we can influence. In a disagreement with our spouse a good rule of thumb is to not bring up past resentments, but rather to stay focused on the current issue, with an emphasis on what can be done in the future to rectify the issue. This approach is consistent with Paul's words to the Philippians:

> Finally, brothers, whatever is true, whatever is noble, whatever is right, whatever is pure, whatever is lovely, whatever is admirable—if anything is excellent or praiseworthy—think about such things. Whatever you have learned or received or heard from me, or seen in me—put into practice. And the God of peace will be with you. (Philippians 4:8-9)

We Pray For Those Who Have Hurt Us

The third aspect of forgiveness is to pray for those who have hurt us. Jesus says, "But I tell you who hear me: Love your enemies, do good to those who hate you, bless those who curse you, pray for those who mistreat you." (Luke 6:27-28) What should we pray for? I believe we should pray for the offender to repent. This will benefit the offender by drawing him or her to God and protect the relationship by making it safer for the hurt party to trust again. It is important to note that forgiveness should not be contingent upon repentance. However, repentance is necessary for reconciliation. We should only reconcile with those who are making an honest effort to stop hurting us. To reconcile prematurely puts ourselves at risk of further injury and demeans our humanity as persons created in God's image.

There are several advantages to this definition of forgiveness because it focuses on actions of the will rather than feelings. The first advantage is that this definition of forgiveness allows us to forgive immediately. Although we cannot immediately *feel* loving toward those who hurt us, we can quickly make a decision to forego retaliation. In addition, this definition permits us to forgive without ignoring our feelings of hurt, betrayal, anger and resentment. This is vital, since our own healing depends on our ability to work through these feelings over a period of weeks, months or, in some cases, even years. Furthermore, defining forgiveness as something we can do through our actions confirms to us that what God commands is possible for us to do. This helps us to not feel guilty or inferior as Christians. Finally, a volitional definition of forgiveness permits us to move forward in our marriages toward the resolution of the conflicts which is one of the best predictors of marital satisfaction.

What Forgiveness Is Not

There are several misconceptions about forgiveness. Here is a list of several things forgiveness is NOT.

1. *Forgiveness is not forgetting.* Because of our human limitations, it is not possible for us to forget the injuries that befall us. God knows us better than

ourselves and wouldn't ask us to forgive unless He knew it was possible. Therefore, forgiveness cannot include forgetting.

2. *Forgiveness does not take away the consequences of the harmful action.* For example, when the prophet Nathan speaks to King David about David's sinful acts (adultery and murder), Nathan says, "The Lord has taken away your sin...but because by doing this you have made the enemies of the Lord show utter contempt, the son born to you will die." (2 Samuel 12:13,14) David did not escape the consequences of his sinful actions.

3. *Forgiveness does not excuse the offense.* When we forgive the offender, we are not saying that what they did was okay. Forgiveness does not mean that we deny or minimize the wound we have suffered or the wrongfulness of the action that caused it.

4. *Forgiveness is not tolerance.* When we forgive, we are not saying that we will continue to put up with the behavior which has hurt us. To the contrary, we pray that the offender will come to repentance. We also set appropriate boundaries to protect ourselves from being hurt again.

5. *Forgiveness is not conditional.* It does not say I can only forgive you if you choose to repent. Rather we forgive regardless of the actions of the offender.

6. *Forgiving does not require us to reconcile with the offender.* Reconciliation is a product of forgiveness and repentance. If there is no repentance, there is no need to reunite with the person who has hurt us. To do so puts us at too much risk of further harm.

Why Forgive?

The first reason we should forgive is that the Bible commands it (Colossians 3:13; Ephesians 4:32). In fact, the Bible tells us that there should be no limit to the number of times we forgive those who have hurt us (Matthew 18:21, 22).

A second reason to forgive is that it helps us heal. Forgiveness is God's gift to us to help us survive the pain inflicted by others. Although the offender is responsible for our injury, we are responsible for our healing. When we refuse to focus on retribution, we are free to pay attention to the myriad of feelings that inevitably accompany our pain. These feelings such as anger, resentment, bitterness and sadness must be felt in a safe environment where their meaning can be fully expressed and understood. Only then can their grip on us loosen and we can free ourselves to be healed.

A third reason to forgive is that our forgiveness combined with the offender's repentance can lead to the restoration of our relationship with the offender. When we forgive our repentant spouse, we restore trust in one another. This enables us to feel safe enough to reconnect with each other in a loving and caring manner.

A final reason to forgive is that forgiveness leads to both physical and psychological benefits. In recent research, forgiveness has been associated with positive health habits (e.g. less smoking), lower anxiety, lower anger, lower depression and better immune system functioning (Seybold, Hill, Neumann & Chi, 2001). In contrast, researchers have found that perpetual hostility is significantly associated with health problems such as coronary heart disease (Miller, Smith, Turner, Guijarro, & Hallet, 1996).

Barriers To Forgiveness

Cunningham (1985) has discussed two barriers to forgiveness. The first barrier is self-righteousness. Cunningham sees our refusal to forgive as an effort to cover feelings of inadequacy and shame with pride and increased self-esteem. Secondly, he feels that we resist forgiveness so that we can continue to manipulate the offender through the induction of guilt.

An additional obstacle to forgiveness is the commonly held assumption that forgiving others is a sign of weakness. The truth is that forgiving takes tremendous courage. When we forgive, we make ourselves vulnerable to further injury. We accept that the fruit of our action is not under our control. Our partner may not choose the path of repentance. Instead, he or she may take advantage of our grace and fail to repent. This is a price we are willing to pay for the opportunity to heal our pain and the possibility of relational reconciliation.

How We Can Forgive

As we receive forgiveness from God, we are empowered to forgive others. Jesus taught us to pray: "Forgive us our debts, as we also have forgiven our debtors." (Matthew 6:12). Forgiveness toward others is intimately connected to our forgiveness from God. Because God is perfect and holy and chooses to forgive us despite our sinfulness, we should be more than willing to forgive others who have hurt us. An illustration can be found in the gospel of John. When Jesus was asked if the woman caught in adultery should be stoned He replied, "If any one of you is without sin, let him be the first to throw a stone at her." (John 8:7)

The same principle applies in marriage. When we are hurt, we first need to humble ourselves before the Lord and remember how fortunate we are to receive His forgiveness. As the Bible says, "The Lord our God is merciful and forgiving even though we have rebelled against him." (Daniel 9:9) We also need to remind ourselves that our spouse is a fallible human being in need of our forgiveness. Finally, we need to remember that God does not expect perfect forgiving. Smedes (2001) has stated, "We are poor duffers trying to treat others as he treats us."

Questions for Reflection:

1. Why is it easier for me to hurt back than to clearly express my hurt?

2. What about this definition of forgiveness will be most difficult for me to follow through on?

3. What misconceptions about forgiveness have I believed?

Weekly Challenge:

When your partner hurts you this week, try to express your hurt rather than hurting back. Notice how this approach affects your relationship.

~ Chapter 6 ~

Empathy

"The purposes of a man's heart are deep waters, but a man of understanding draws them out." (Proverbs 20:5)

"Understanding is a fountain of life to those who have it." (Proverbs 16:22a)

"My dear brothers, take note of this: Everyone should be quick to listen, slow to speak and slow to become angry." (James 1:19)

Empathy is one of the greatest gifts we can give to our spouse. As a psychotherapist for a number of years, I have learned to never underestimate the value of taking a genuine interest in the life of another. Time and time again clients have told me that the most beneficial aspect of their counseling experience has been the feeling of being truly understood. Conversely, many of my clients have initially come to therapy with overwhelming feelings of isolation and loneliness. I have all too often heard the lament, "No one cares or understands."

Marriages, like other intimate relationships, greatly benefit from the expression of empathy. Research has shown that marital happiness is positively correlated with perceived empathy (Rowan, Compton & Rust, 1995). Davis and Oathout (1987) have found that empathy is one of the most important ways of maintaining the quality of relationships. Lauer, Lauer, and Kerr (1990) have found that marital satisfaction correlates with the understanding and acceptance of the views and needs of one's spouse.

Empathy allows love to be felt in the deep places of one's heart and soul. Empathy heals hurts. It soothes pains. It comforts and transforms those whom it touches. Empathy binds couples together. It frees spouses to share their deepest fears and longings. One can never underestimate the power of empathy. It builds trust, increases warmth and enhances intimacy.

Dr. Paul Tournier (1967) has written beautifully on the value of empathy:

> You well know that beautiful prayer of Francis of Assisi: 'Lord! Grant that I may seek more to understand than to be understood...' It is this new desire which the Holy Spirit awakens in couples and which transforms their marriage. As long as a man is preoccupied primarily with being understood by his wife, he is miserable, overcome with self-pity, the spirit of demanding, and bitter withdrawal. As soon as he becomes preoccupied with understanding her, seeking to understand that

which he had not before understood, and with his own wrongdoing in not having understood her, then the direction taken by events begins to change. As soon as a person feels understood, he opens up, and because he lowers his defenses he is also able to make himself better understood (p.29).

What Is Empathy?

I define empathy as the ability to understand the internal experience of another and to communicate that understanding in a way in which the other person feels genuinely cared for.

Practical Principles For Expressing Empathy

Understanding the internal experience of one's spouse is not an easy task. Communicating that understanding can be even more difficult. There are often several thoughts, feelings and associated meanings occupying the mind of one's spouse at any given moment. The following are practical principles for gaining a better understanding of your spouse and communicating that understanding in an effective manner.

Listen With Genuine Interest

Some people say that God gives us two ears and one mouth for a reason. It is better to listen than to speak. Proverbs 18.13 says, "He who answers before listening—that is his folly and his shame." Good listeners do not interrupt. They make sure they get the whole story before they respond. They encourage further disclosure by making comments such as, "Is there anything else you would like to say?"

Furthermore, good listeners take a sincere interest in what their spouse is saying and feeling. They do not feign interest. They do not patronize. Rather, they find something interesting in what they are hearing. Good listeners summarize in their mind what they are hearing rather than mentally preparing a response. They drop what they are doing to listen. This means turning away from the television or computer. It means putting down the newspaper or magazine. It means looking at our partner as we listen rather than focusing on the unfolded laundry. It even means that we may have to ask our children to wait for our attention until we finish a conversation with our spouse.

Finally, good listeners vary their facial expressions and vocal intonations. These non-verbal signs of interest often have a more powerful effect than the actual words spoken.

Ask Clarifying Questions

In order to fully understand one's spouse, it is often necessary to ask clarifying questions. Some examples include: "What happened?" "What do you mean by that?" "Can you clarify what you just said?" "What prompted you to say that?" or "Why did you respond that way?" These questions invite elaboration which, in turn, enhances understanding.

*Go Beyond The Content Of The Words
Spoken To Gain Understanding*

In his article on effective listening, Paul Blodgett (1997) has wisely stated, "A good listener knows that the words we use, even when carefully chosen, often represent little more than a rough attempt to communicate what we really mean (p.11).

In my private practice, I frequently meet couples who communicate in very different ways. For example, a common problem involves spouses who want to communicate a particular feeling and do so by making overgeneralizations, empty threats and false accusations. Their spouses, however, don't see these words as mere symbolic expressions of strong feelings but rather take them literally and feel hurt, criticized and mistreated. The hurt spouses then generally respond by defending, counterattacking or withdrawing. At this point, I encourage the offended spouses to not take the words literally and to try and grasp the feelings their spouse is attempting to verbalize. I also ask the spouse sending the message to try and use more precise language to convey their feelings. Most importantly, I inform the couple that the incident is an example of poor communication and not an indicator of a lack of love, care or concern.

*Ask Your Spouse To Share His Or
Her Thoughts And Feelings*

It may sound simple, but great questions to ask include: "What were you thinking?" "How are you feeling?" "What were you feeling" or "How did that affect you?" These questions encourage spouses to reflect on their experience at a level beyond the details of what happened and to focus on their own unique perceptions and reactions.

Show Sensitivity

Sensitivity can be shown by communicating to one's spouse the understanding that has been gained. Make comments such as: "That must have been exciting," "I'll bet that hurt your feelings," "I can see how you could be frustrated by that" or "I'm sure that was hard to take." These comments let spouses know that their experiences are understood and worth noting. Remember that sensitivity to positive experiences can be just as important as sensitivity to negative experiences. If spouses are only given attention when they are sad, troubled, worried or frustrated, they may infer that they are only worthy of attention when things go wrong. This can lead to an increase in self-defeating behavior.

Validate The Experience Of Your Spouse

Two simple statements can show spouses how much their feelings and thoughts matter. They are: "I can understand why you think/feel this way" and "That makes sense to me." Note that these statements convey understanding and acceptance but not necessarily agreement. The following is an example of sensitivity and validation without agreement:

> Wife: Your mother doesn't like my cooking.

Husband: What happened? (question for clarification)
Wife: She told me not to cook anything for the party this Saturday.
Husband: How did you feel when she said that? (question to elicit feeling)
Wife: It hurt my feelings, and I feel like she thinks I'm a bad wife because I don't cook as well as she does.
Husband: It must be frustrating to feel like you don't measure up to her no matter how hard you try. (sensitivity)
Wife: You got it.
Husband: It makes sense to me that you feel so frustrated.
Wife: Do you really think I'm that bad of a cook?
Husband: No, I think you're a great cook, and I think my mother does too. I think she was just trying to be nice and give you a break. After all, you have been working very hard lately, and she probably doesn't want to add another thing to your plate.
Wife: Maybe you're right. I'll give her a call and tell her I appreciate her concern, but I really would love to at least make a cake.
Husband: That sounds like a great idea.

Find The Meanings Associated With The Thoughts And Feelings

Each perception, thought and feeling will inevitably have an associated meaning that is idiosyncratic to each spouse.

The empathic spouse persistently seeks these personalized meanings by asking specific questions designed to elicit meaning. One effective question is simply, "What does it mean to you?" Another question might be, "What was your interpretation/impression of what that meant?" Here is an example of a conversation where meaning is sought:

> Husband: My boss is leaving town tomorrow.
> Wife: What happened? (getting the story)
> Husband: He has to attend a conference in Arizona for a week.
> Wife: So, what does this mean? (question to elicit meaning)
> Husband: It means that I've got twice as much work next week.
> Wife: Sounds like you've got a long week ahead of you. (sensitivity)
> Husband: Yeah, and I probably won't make John's hockey game on Tuesday, which really bums me out.
> Wife: That makes sense to me. I know how much you love to watch his games, and I know how much he enjoys having you there. (sensitivity and validation)
> Husband: Yeah. (shrugs his shoulders and sighs deeply).
> Wife: Missing John's game seems to really upset you. (sensitivity) What does it mean to you when you miss a game? (question to elicit meaning)
> Husband: It really bothers me because my parents came to all my games when I was a kid, and I know how much that meant to me. I told myself I would be

the same with my children, and I feel like I'm not only letting John down, but I feel like I'm letting myself down too.

Wife: I can understand that, and I know it isn't easy for you to miss even a single game, but I really think John will understand. Maybe when your boss comes back you can get off early one day and take John to the hockey rink. I'm sure he would enjoy that. (validation)

Husband: That sounds like a great idea.

Summarize What You Have Learned About Your Spouse

After you have listened carefully, shown sensitivity, validated experiences and explored deeper meanings, it can be very helpful to summarize what you have learned. This is the time to speak concisely, coherently and accurately. For example, you could say, "It sounds to me like you've had a long day at work, and that means you would love to go to bed early tonight. I can really understand that. It also sounds like it means a lot for you to go to David's recital tonight so the sleep is just going to have to wait." When this kind of summary is given with a congruent tone of voice and facial expressions, a feeling of relaxation can usually be noticed by the spouse on the receiving end. Receiving that kind of empathy is like drinking ice-cold lemonade on a balmy summer day.

Check For Accuracy

The final step in the process of empathy is to check for understanding. This can be as simple as asking, "Am I getting it?" or "Does it seem to you that I understand?" If the answer is yes, reward yourself for a job well done.

Questions for Reflection:

1. What does it mean to you when you feel understood by your partner?

2. What can you do to improve your ability to empathize with your partner?

3. From your perspective, how can your partner improve their ability to empathize?

Weekly Challenge:

Pick any conversation with your partner this week and attempt to listen empathically, rather than offering advice, attempting to solve a problem or giving unsolicited feedback. Note how your partner responds. Did they seem to relax when you summarized your understanding of what they were going through? When you asked, did they tell you that they felt understood?

~ Chapter 7 ~

Respect

"Show proper respect to everyone." (1 Peter 2:17a)

"Husbands, in the same way be considerate as you live with your wives, and treat them with respect..." (1Peter 3:7a)

"However, each one of you also must love his wife as he loves himself, and the wife must respect her husband." (Ephesians 5:33)

"Be devoted to one another in brotherly love. Honor one another above yourselves." (Romans 12:10)

Respect typically abounds in new marriages. Sadly, it also tends to subside as marriages mature. Dissatisfied couples inadvertently feed disrespect by taking each other for granted as they grow more comfortable with one another over time. Gradually, respect fades as couples stop doing the little things that communicate respect in concrete ways. On the other hand, satisfied couples realize that respect must remain consistent and constant regardless of how comfortable they feel with their spouse. These couples routinely expend the time and energy necessary to keep respect alive and well.

How can spouses show respect to each other? Here are some practical ideas: Opening doors, buying meaningful gifts, celebrating fine performances, saying thank you, showing affection in public, checking in with each other at social gatherings, listening attentively, working together to make a decision, spending money wisely, praising each other liberally, avoiding harsh words, saying excuse me, asking for an opinion, coming home on time, including each other in leisure activities, learning from each other, writing notes of appreciation, planning a special night out, disclosing intimate thoughts and feelings, canceling previous plans in order to comfort a spouse in need and openly expressing pride and admiration for one another.

As the above list shows, respect can be shown in a variety of ways. The reality of married life however, is that we know what we ought to do, but we sometimes don't feel like doing it. We need to find ways to keep our motivation to serve and respect one another fresh and alive. In the paragraphs that follow, I will discuss several ways we can restore our desire to show respect to our spouse on a regular basis.

Be Romantic

Nothing can improve a relationship quicker than a little romance. I'm sure most wives would agree that a romantic act can cover a multitude of sins. The following is just a small list of romantic ideas: Write love letters to each other, leave loving text messages, buy thoughtful gifts, plan and go out on dates, spend time together without the children, go away for the weekend, take a walk, plan a special evening together at home, light candles, play together, take a bath together, read a book together, watch a sunset, reenact special dates you have been on in the past, talk to each other in quiet places, touch base throughout the day and laugh together. I'm sure there are many more you can think of. Use your imagination, and I'm sure you can come up with many more romantic ideas.

There are three keys to reviving romance in your relationship. First of all, find out what feels romantic to your spouse. Their feedback will likely highlight similarities and reveal important differences. Second, do things that are innovative and creative. Avoid getting into ruts by keeping things fresh and varied. Finally, push yourself outside of your comfort zone in order to put new ideas into practice.

Show Appreciation

I have never met a spouse who has felt over appreciated. Appreciation is a simple and yet powerful way to build trust and intimacy in marriage. Couples who focus on mutual appreciation will find numerous opportunities to compliment or praise one another. A spouse can be appreciated for anything from how hard they work to how fun they are to play with. Sadly, words and acts of appreciation are too often forgotten or put off when the urgent but not always important demands of daily life get in the way. Therefore, we need to force ourselves to express appreciation as often as possible. The consequences of adding appreciation to a marriage can be pleasantly surprising. When couples feel important and valued, they often increase their own acts of kindness, consideration and respect. This in turn leads to more positive feelings and behavior.

One common fallacy couples often share is the belief that appreciation should not be given until it is received in order to maintain one's sense of dignity. I disagree. The best path to take for the sake of the relationship is to appreciate one another without regard to the consequences of the action. In other words, it is best to love unconditionally. This is the way God has loved us and urges us to love others. John 15:12 says, "My command is this: Love each other as I have loved you."

A second fallacy regarding appreciation is that the broader the appreciation, the better. Again, I disagree. It is far more effective to be specific and precise rather than general when offering words of thankfulness. For example, a comment like, "You are great" is nice, but not as meaningful as "I really appreciate you doing the dishes last night." The former comment could be interpreted as shallow and empty, while the latter comment is more likely to be viewed as genuine gratitude.

Complement Each Other

The Bible says, "Pleasant words are a honeycomb, sweet to

the soul and healing to the bones." (Proverbs 16:24) Proverbs 25:11 also states, "A word aptly spoken is like apples of gold in settings of silver." Compliments demonstrate respect by letting spouses know how much they are treasured and cherished. Compliments also increase respect by conveying feelings of admiration and positive regard.

Compliments are best received when they are genuine and realistic. For example, an unrealistic compliment such as, "You are the most attractive woman in the world" is not as effective as "You look beautiful in that new dress." The former compliment is so outlandish that it is not likely to be seen as sincere; however, the latter compliment is realistic, and therefore, is more likely to produce a positive response. Furthermore, the former compliment is akin to what the Bible denounces as flattery. Proverbs 26:28 proclaims, "A lying tongue hates those it hurts, and a flattering mouth works ruin."

One of the keys to successful complimenting is to keep compliments fresh and diverse. This might be a struggle for some couples. One effective strategy is to think of an annoying characteristic of your spouse and then think about what a positive aspect of that very same characteristic might be. For instance, take the spouse who is viewed as obsessive and compulsive. This same spouse can be complimented for being organized and efficient. Or, take the spouse who is viewed as irresponsible, impulsive and childish. This spouse can be complimented for being spontaneous, playful and fun to be with.

Value Differences

The old adage that "opposites attract" is true for most couples. More than likely, couples realize early on in their marriages how different they are from their spouse. The existence of differences in marriage is not a problem. Problems only arise when the differences are not handled with acceptance and are viewed as sources of excessive irritation and annoyance.

On the other hand, differences are necessary for the growth and development of each marital partner. Spouses should not be criticized for being different. Furthermore, a spouse should not focus on changing his or her partner to fit a personal agenda for how life ought to be lived. Rather, spouses should view one another as vessels through which God can teach us to become more like Christ. Satisfied couples understand that they can become more balanced and well rounded by learning from each other. When differences are viewed in this manner, couples are free to become all that God has created them to be.

In my role as a clinical psychologist, I tell couples that God has brought them together to complement one another and to help each other grow. After all, Genesis 2:18 says, "It is not good for the man to be alone. I will make a helper suitable for him." The following example illustrates how couples can complement each other and facilitate positive growth through their personality differences:

John and Lisa have been married for five years. John's

chief complaints boil down to his belief that Lisa treats him like a child. Lisa's complaints boil down to her belief that John acts like a child and gives her no choice but to parent him. As I work with this couple, I will encourage John to take life more seriously, to follow through on his commitments, to stop blaming others for his own shortcomings and to increase his acts of service toward Lisa. I will tell him that he can benefit by becoming more like Lisa and developing his ability to be more reliable, responsible, organized and productive. On the other hand, I will encourage Lisa to be more relaxed, less critical of John, to ask for help, to take better care of herself and to include John in decision-making. I will tell Lisa that she can benefit by becoming more like John and developing her ability to be playful, spontaneous, relaxed and accepting.

When differences among spouses are valued, couples live in synchrony with the Biblical concept of a composite unity made up of several parts all of equal importance and value. Paul illustrates this concept in his words to the Corinthians, who quarreled over the value of one spiritual gift over another:

> Now the body is not made up of one part but of many. If the foot should say, 'Because I am not a hand, I do not belong to the body,' it would not for that reason cease to be part of the body...But in fact God has arranged the parts in the body, every one of them, just as he wanted them to be...The eye cannot say to the

hand, 'I don't need you!' And the head cannot say to the feet, 'I don't need you!' (1 Corinthians 12:14-21)

Marriage, like the Church body, is a composite unity made up of different and yet equally valuable parts. The Bible teaches in Genesis that the husband and wife are two distinct persons who become united as one flesh (Genesis 2:24). Therefore, each spouse needs to be valued and respected as an equally important part of the union God has created. Paul has written, "If one part is honored, every part rejoices with it." (1 Corinthians 12:26)

Restrain Your Anger

The Bible states, "A fool gives full vent to his anger, but a wise man keeps himself under control." (Proverbs 29:11) Respectful spouses attempt to control their tongue. They understand that, "A gentle answer turns away wrath, but a harsh word stirs up anger." (Proverbs 15:1) A commonly held misconception is the belief, "If I feel it then I should say it." This is not true. The Bible encourages us to exercise self-control as when we speak to our spouse, regardless of how angry we might be. James speaks directly to this point, "If anyone considers himself religious and yet does not keep a tight rein on his tongue, he deceives himself and his religion is worthless." (James 1:26)

Put Each Other First

Couples who respect each other will place each other at the top of their priority list. The Bible seems to affirm the need to place one's spouse higher on the priority list than one's parents. Genesis 2:24 says, "For this reason a man will leave his father and mother and be united to his wife, and they will become one flesh." Thus, spouses need to stand up for each other even if it means standing against their parents. To stand up for one's parents over and against one's spouse indicates that a true "leaving" has not occurred. Furthermore, I believe spouses should be a higher priority than children. I have seen far too many marriages fail because of a lack of attention to the needs of the marriage coupled with too much attention paid to the children. I understand this is a controversial position, but I firmly believe the best gift a parent can give their children is a happy marriage filled with love and respect.

Questions for Reflection:

1. What are some specific things your partner can do to enhance romance in your relationship?

2. What do you appreciate about your partner?

3. What are some strengths of your partner's personality that you would like to develop in your own personality?

Weekly Challenge:

Plan a romantic time with your partner this week. While you are together give each other at least one compliment and one word of appreciation. Discuss how it feels to receive compliments and words of appreciation.

~ Chapter 8 ~

Intimacy

"The Lord God said, 'It is not good for the man to be alone. I will make a helper suitable for him.'" (Genesis 2:18)

"For this reason a man will leave his father and mother and be united to his wife, and they will become one flesh." (Genesis 2:24)

The Biblical phrase "one flesh" beautifully describes the intimacy found in healthy marriages. It is a Hebrew idiom that implies a comprehensive and seamless union between husband and wife. It refers to a bond characterized by psychological, relational, physical and spiritual oneness. The purpose of this chapter is to offer concrete and practical ways of enhancing and deepening intimacy at each of these four levels.

Psychological Intimacy

The best means of building psychological intimacy is through genuine self-disclosure. Researchers have found that greater depth of self-disclosure is positively correlated with increased intimacy (Waring, Schaefer, & Fry, 1994).

I define self-disclosure as an open and honest expression of one's thoughts, feelings, beliefs, values and attitudes. Furthermore, self-disclosure is done best in a spirit of authenticity and vulnerability.

Husbands and wives often feel conflicted when it comes to self-disclosure. A part of them wants to know and be known at the deepest parts. This makes perfect sense since God created us to be relationally connected. The Bible tells us that even before sin entered the world it was, "Not good for man to be alone." (Genesis 2:18) The Bible also tells us that Adam and Eve were, "Naked and not ashamed." (Genesis 2:25) As God's children we long to feel naked and not ashamed with one another.

Unfortunately, Adam and Eve did not stay naked and without shame for very long. They rebelled against God and sin entered the world. As soon as this happened, they felt ashamed in their nakedness and hid themselves with fig leaves. From this time on, it has been difficult for man and woman to be *naked* with each other because they fear that their openness will result in feelings of shame just like Adam and Eve.

In a sinful world, we fear that honest and open self-disclosure may upset our spouse. We worry that they may respond in a hurtful manner when we psychologically undress in their presence. We fear their disappointment, rejection, and in some cases, even their abandonment. We fear that we will end up feeling anxious, ashamed, alone, guilty and inadequate.

In order to protect themselves from the potential undesirable consequences of self-disclosure, spouses often hide their true selves from one another. Spouses can hide in a variety of ways. Here are just a few: staying busy, staying quiet, changing the subject, speaking generally, keeping conversations superficial, gossiping about others, focusing on the children, watching television, surfing the internet and giving vague and/or short answers to questions.

The problem with hiding is that it really doesn't work. It can only protect us from pain by cutting off our access to intimacy. Self-disclosure is the road to psychological intimacy, and when that road is closed, the destination can no longer be reached. If we continually avoid self-disclosure, our relationship will eventually die a quiet death. Thus, we really have no choice. We must push past our fears. Despite the very real risks, we must find the courage to share our innermost thoughts and feelings with our spouse.

Such boldness is only possible when we rely on God to meet our needs for safety, security and significance. We need to remind ourselves what God has done and continues to do for us. When we feel anxious, God gives us peace. When we feel guilty, He forgives us. When we feel ashamed and inferior, He reminds us of our value and worth, and when we feel alone, He comforts us with His loving presence.

Because of our secure relationship with our heavenly Father, we can afford to take risks in our earthly relationships. The good news is that in Christian marriage the risk is not as great as one might think. Just as we are called to pursue oneness by risking self-disclosure, the receiver of our self-disclosure is called by God to pursue oneness by responding to us with compassion and empathy rather than judgment and condemnation. When each spouse is empowered by the Holy Spirit to do their part, the longing for nakedness without shame can be satisfied.

Appropriate Self-Disclosure

Self-disclosure is an excellent way to increase intimacy with another person. Paul writes in his letter to the Thessalonians, "We loved you so much that we were delighted to share with you not only the gospel of God but our lives as well because you had become so dear to us." (1 Thessalonians 2:8) When we are transparent with our spouse, we allow our relationship to move to a deeper level. As we become more known to one another, we become closer. It doesn't matter what we share as long as we share truthfully and openly.

Self-disclosure is not easy. There are risks involved. When we bear our souls to another, we run the risk of being hurt. When our self-revelations are not handled with care and compassion, we can feel deeply rejected. Therefore, when our spouse is self-disclosing to us, we need to remain attentive, respectful and encouraging. We should never use their disclosures to exact revenge when we feel wronged. We should never minimize or deny the strength of their feelings. We should never disregard their ideas and opinions because we think they are illogical or disorganized. Rather, we need to provide a safe and secure climate for our spouses to explore and express all aspects of their being.

Self-disclosure must be appropriate. We need to balance our need for intimacy with our partner's need to be treated with respect and dignity. It's not okay to tell your wife her thighs look heavier, or to tell your husband you think he has the common sense of a child. There are some things best left unsaid.

Relational Intimacy

This refers to the degree to which we feel emotionally connected to our partner. There is a sense of closeness and comfortableness when we are talking, playing or just hanging out together. We can count on each other in times of need. We can speak to each other and know that our confidences will be kept. We function as a unit, and we are willing to sacrifice our own self-interests for the sake of the team.

Relational intimacy also refers to our ability to enjoy each other's company. We love spending time together. We have common interests that we enjoy participating in together. We can laugh together, play together, cry together and dream together. We are best friends.

Physical Intimacy

This area of intimacy is often neglected by couples, especially those who have been married for a while. However, it is vitally important to keep the fire of passion alive and well throughout our marriages.

The Bible has a high view of sexual passion in marriage. Song of Songs speaks frequently and positively about the wonders and joys of sexual passion in marriage. Here is a brief excerpt from this eloquent and poetic tribute to passion and physical desire:

> How beautiful your sandaled feet, O prince's daughter!
> Your graceful legs are like jewels, the work of a craftsman's hands.
> Your navel is a rounded goblet that never lacks blended wine.
> Your waist is a mound of wheat encircled by lilies,
> Your breasts are like two fawns, twins of a gazelle.
> (Song of Songs 7:1-3)

Later in this passage we read this:

> I said, 'I will climb the palm tree; I will take hold of its fruit.'
> May your breasts be like the clusters of the vine, the fragrance of your breath like apples, and the mouth like the best wine.
> May the wine go straight to my lover, flowing gently over lips and teeth. (Song of Songs 7:8-9)

The apostle Paul spoke about the importance of fulfilling each other's sexual needs in his first letter to the Corinthians:

> But since there is so much immorality, each man should have his own wife and each woman her own husband. The husband should fulfill his marital duty to his wife, and likewise the wife to her husband. The wife's body does not belong to her alone but also to her husband. In the same way, the husband's body does not belong to him alone but also to his wife. (1 Corinthians 7:2-4)

One of the great mysteries of marriage is that God has made men and women different sexually. We are not only different anatomically, but also emotionally and psychologically. You have probably heard the saying, "Men are like microwaves and women are like slow cookers." In other words, men heat up very fast with sexual desire whereas women require more time. For men, sex starts in the bedroom. For women it may start at breakfast. A pleasant and intimate conversation can sexually arouse a woman as much as physical foreplay. In addition, small gestures of physical affection throughout the day can greatly enhance a wife's sexual interest. Holding hands, hugging and kissing are things that many women in my office plead for from their husbands.

In my practice, husbands and wives often have the same complaint, "We don't have enough intimacy." The problem is that they are talking about two entirely different things. Men are saying, "I want more sexual intercourse." Women are saying, "I want more conversation, more romance, more affection, more foreplay and more sexual intercourse." It's not that women don't want to enjoy sex; it's just that they want it to be more comprehensive. Husbands who get this are much more likely to have a satisfying sex life. Their commitment to meeting their wives' broad-based sexual needs will be richly rewarded in the bedroom.

Spiritual Intimacy

This is probably the most crucial area of intimacy for a Christian couple. You have probably heard the saying, "The couple that prays together stays together." Research by Greeley (1991) has found incredible support for this notion. In his analysis of 657 couples throughout the United States, Greeley found that 90% of couples who prayed together and were sexually satisfied reported feeling very happy in their marriage. Furthermore, 60% of couples who were not sexually satisfied but still prayed together reported feeling very happy with their marriage.

Prayer has several benefits for couples. Most importantly, prayer is a powerful means by which we invite God to participate in our marriage. The acknowledgement of His presence can lead to an increased sense of safety and security, which allows us to relate to each other with authenticity, honesty and vulnerability. If we know God will catch us if our spouse fails us, it becomes much easier to jump into the arms of our spouse. This kind of trust and vulnerability leads to increased feelings of tenderness, closeness and connectedness with one another.

Prayer gives us hope in the midst of despair, wisdom when indecision abounds, courage in the face of adversity, peace when anxiety overwhelms us and comfort when we suffer. Prayer helps us to feel secure and safe as we remember that God is in control, and He is on our side. Prayer helps us to humble ourselves and to be honest. When we pray to the God who knows everything, there is no need to hide or to put up a front. It is healthy for our spouse to hear us relate to God in such a vulnerable, humble and dependent manner. This helps us grow in empathy and understanding for one another and leads to greater feelings of closeness and compassion.

Other means of increasing spiritual intimacy include the following: Bible study, devotions, church attendance and listening to inspirational music. In addition, time spent talking about our personal spiritual journeys with our spouse can greatly enhance intimacy. I encourage you to find what works best for you as a couple. There are several resources available to you at your local Christian bookstore.

Questions for Reflection:

1. What do I need to disclose to my partner that I haven't yet done?

2. What are some ways we as a couple could enhance our spiritual intimacy?

3. How do we feel about praying together out loud? How does my own pride, fear of vulnerability and self-dependence get in the way?

Weekly Challenge:

Spend time together discussing your spiritual journeys up to this point. Notice how close you feel after doing this.

~ Chapter 9 ~

Patience

"Love is patient…" (1 Corinthians 13:4)

"Be completely humble and gentle; be patient, bearing with one another in love." (Ephesians 4:2)

"A hot-tempered man stirs up dissension, but a patient man calms a quarrel." (Proverbs 15:18)

In our current culture of fast food, overnight delivery and smart phones, the virtue of patience is becoming increasingly rare. Nevertheless, in marriage it remains crucially important. Couples who are patient can weather the storms of conflict, extend much needed grace to one another and sustain their hope despite temporary disappointments.

The research on patience has demonstrated the value of this undervalued and underutilized virtue. Patience has been found to act as an antidote to anger, aggression and depression (Leifer, 1996), and a correlate of optimism (Hooda, 2009), cooperation (Curry, 2008) and spiritual transcendence (Emmons, 2007).

What Is Patience?

I define patience as waiting for what you desire, extending grace unconditionally and continually doing what is right even when there is no immediate reward. Patient spouses are, "Quick to listen, slow to speak and slow to become angry." (James 1:19) They endure suffering for the sake of a greater long-term good. They have mastered the art of tolerating frustration and delaying gratification.

Willing To Wait For What You Desire

The Bible testifies that good things come to those who wait:

> Be patient, then brothers, until the Lord's coming. See how the farmer waits for the land to yield its valuable crop and how patient he is for the autumn and spring rains. You too, be patient and stand firm. (James 5:7-8)

In marriage, the sanctification and transformation of our spouse is God's business, not ours. And God knows best. He knows how and when to initiate the process of character development. We are much better off if we wait on the Lord and stop trying to change our spouse with our own schemes and strategies. Paradoxically, when we stop trying to force change in our spouses, they feel more relaxed and comfortable to make the changes we desire.

It is important to remember that we need to wait as long as the Lord wills, not as long as we think we can endure. We are wise to remember that Abraham waited patiently for 25 years to receive his promised son (Hebrews 6:13-15).

Extending Grace Unconditionally

Extending grace unconditionally means offering grace even when our spouses are too weak to extend grace themselves, or they try to extend grace with limited success, or they simply refuse to extend grace. During these times we must remember that God is extremely patient with us despite our foolishness, rebelliousness and disobedience (2 Peter 3:9). And He wants us to reflect His love to our spouse by doing likewise. In his letter to the Thessalonians, Paul writes, "Live in peace with each other. And we urge you brothers, warn those who are idle, encourage the timid, help the weak, be patient with everyone." (1 Thessalonians 5:13-14)

Notice in this passage that Paul associates peace with patience. When we are patient, we experience greater peace in our marriages. When we take the high road of patience instead of demanding immediate gratification, we love our spouse in a manner that promotes harmony. Unilateral grace has the power to disarm defenses, deescalate anger and foster calmness in the midst of disappointment and distress.

Doing What Is Right Relentlessly

Another important aspect of patience is continually doing what is right in the eyes of God, regardless of the outcome. In other words, we need to continue to behave toward our spouse in ways that God prescribes, even when we see no progress or reward for our actions. Paul exhorts us to be patient in affliction (Romans 12:12) and to have endurance when things aren't necessarily going our way (Colossians 1:11).

I often counsel couples who come back one week after I have prescribed a new way of relating to one another with a deflated and defeated attitude. When I ask what is wrong, they typically respond by saying, "Dr. Mendez, we tried your suggestion, but it doesn't work." I then ask them how they know it hasn't worked. They answer by lamenting on how their new behavior was not rewarded by an immediate and positive change in their spouse.

In these situations, I remind couples that change usually does not occur in an atmosphere lacking in trust and safety, and that trust and safety only develop through repeated and numerous positive interactions. I also tell couples that they need to begin defining "success" in terms of how well they are executing God's game plan for their marriage rather than how rewarding their spouse's reaction is toward them. I explain that when you sail a ship, it is possible to remain exactly on course even when the ocean looks the same today as it did yesterday and there is no land in sight.

How To Be Patient

Patience is not easy, but it can be developed by consistently devoting ourselves to prayer and by changing the way we think. First of all, we cannot put this definition of patience into practice on our own. Paul states that patience flows from being strengthened by God who is almighty (Colossians 1:11). We need to pray for God's strength in every situation where patience is needed.

Secondly, the Bible says that we can be, "Transformed by the renewing of our mind." (Romans 12:2) Therefore, we need to think clear and truthful thoughts. Here are some examples of transforming thoughts regarding patience:

> *"A good marriage can be an imperfect marriage."*
>
> *"My spouse's reactions do not define the value of my behavior."*
>
> *"God is faithful and will transform my spouse according to His purposes in His perfect timing."*
>
> *"Patience leads to peace."*
>
> *"God gives me patience when I am filled with His spirit."*

As I have mentioned, patience is not popular these days. Patience is difficult to exhibit, and it often goes unnoticed and unrewarded. Nevertheless, patience remains a virtue that promotes peace and contentment in marriage.

Questions for Reflection:

1. When is it hard to wait? What is hard to wait for?

2. Share of an area of your relationship where you need grace. Share an area of your relationship where you can extend grace.

3. Give an example from your life where patient endurance is needed. What will help you to continue to patiently endure?

Weekly Challenge:

Extend grace to your partner this week unconditionally and unilaterally. At the end of the week, share with your spouse what you did and when you did it. Ask them if they noticed and if so, how they felt about it.

~ CHAPTER 10 ~

Kindness

"Therefore as God's chosen people, holy and dearly loved, clothe yourselves with compassion, kindness, humility, gentleness and patience." (Colossians 3:12)

"An anxious heart weighs a man down, but a kind word cheers him up." (Proverbs 12:25)

What Is Kindness?

Kindness is the warm, authentic and generous extension of care and compassion for the purpose of encouraging another without expecting anything in return. In marriage, true kindness often leads to feelings of gratitude and fondness. Kindness has the power to heal brokenness, repair ruptures of attachment and foster intimacy and mutual attraction.

The Bible refers to kindness as an aspect of love (1 Corinthians 13:4-7) and a fruit of the Spirit (Galatians 5:22). Kindness flows when we allow God's love to penetrate and emanate from our hearts and when we ask the Holy Spirit to fill us with His power and presence.

Research has shown that happy people score higher on scores of the recognition and enactment of kind behaviors (Otake, 2006). In addition, psychologists have discovered that happy people report feeling more kind just by counting their acts of kindness (Otake, 2006).

There are a variety of ways couples can express kindness. Examples of kindness in marriage include the following: Words of support and comfort, words of encouragement, service and giving.

Words Of Support

Words of support and comfort provide a secure base and a safe haven to one's spouse. Proverbs 16:24 states, "Pleasant words are a honeycomb, sweet to the soul and healing to the bones." When a spouse feels hurt, broken and beat up by the demands of life, a word of kindness can function as a healing balm. Usually, kind words are not advice, quick fixes or shallow praises aimed at removing pain. Rather, they are deeply felt and empathic words of understanding that comfort our spouses in the midst of their pain.

Words Of Encouragement

Proverbs 18:21 states, "The tongue has the power of life and death." Words cannot only dampen relational satisfaction, but they can also destroy one's spirit. On the other hand, Proverbs 25:11 teaches, "A word aptly spoken is like apples of gold in settings of silver." There are all kinds of words and phrases that communicate encouragement. We encourage when we tell our spouses how much we believe in them and how confident we are in their abilities. We extend kindness through words when we admire our spouses' tenacity, appreciate their patience, respect their work ethic and value their love for Christ.

Service

In the book of Ephesians, Paul writes, "Serve wholeheartedly, as if you were serving the Lord, not men." (Ephesians 6:7) Our service to our spouse is more likely to reflect kindness when we serve one another as if we are serving the Lord. Paul has written that service is an antidote to "biting and devouring." (Galatians 5:13-15) Thus, couples can escape destructive cycles of criticism and defensiveness by focusing on service rather than selfish desires.

The positive value of service is always defined by the receiver, not the giver. Too often spouses fall into the common trap of serving their spouse in ways they would like to be served. Serving wisely is like buying a good birthday present. The best gifts are the ones your spouse has hinted to you he or she would enjoy and treasure, not the present you think they desire just because you like it.

Therefore, when we serve, it is important to be mindful of what our spouse truly desires and finds meaningful. I recommend that couples work smart in their marriages rather than working hard. When wives serve in ways that result in husband's feeling important, respected and admired, they are working smart. When husbands serve in ways that result in their wives feeling cherished, treasured and secure, they are also working wisely.

Giving

Jesus said, "Freely you have received, freely give." (Matthew 10:8) Here, Jesus reminds us that just as God gives freely, we ought to as well. This means that we give in marriage without expecting anything in return. This is impossible to do on our own, but it is a natural consequence of experiencing the undeserved gift of grace bestowed upon us by our heavenly Father.

Paul extends our Christian understanding of helpful giving by writing, "God loves a cheerful giver." (2 Corinthians 9:7) This means that we are better off not giving at all, as opposed to giving with resentment in our hearts. Husbands and wives do not help their marriages when they give grudgingly. However, when spouses give freely and cheerfully, marriages are strengthened. Paul writes that "Kindness leads to repentance." (Romans 2:4) The truth is that we can elicit genuine sorrow and commitments to change when we extend a gift of kindness toward our spouses, especially when they don't deserve it. The irony is that many couples refuse to extend kindness when they feel they are owed an apology. This tactic only serves to steal from them that which they seek.

False Kindness

Even though certain actions may feel kind to the giver, they may not be in the long-term best interests of the receiver. I call these gestures "false kindness." I see five common types of false kindness in my clinical practice: Flattery, giving up one's convictions, enabling dysfunctional behavior, empty words and quick advice.

Flattery

According to the Bible, "A flattering mouth works ruin." (Proverbs 26:28) Flattery is harmful because the recipient does not feel affirmed when the compliment given does not resonate as congruent with reality. Rather, the recipients may feel offended if they think the flatterer is trying to control them or gain their favor by such disingenuous remarks. In marriage, compliments and affirmations are helpful only when they are sincere, specific and accurate. I encourage couples in my practice to share whatever positive thoughts they have about their spouse throughout the day either by e-mail, text message or a phone call. However, I strongly discourage the artificial manufacturing of positive words that satisfy self-interest more than the well-being of their spouse.

Giving Up One's Convictions

It is noble and healthy to have the courage to stand up for one's convictions. Unfortunately, many spouses too easily relinquish their convictions these days, because they falsely believe it is kind to do so. For example, if a wife believes that family members should speak truthfully, it is not kind, but rather detrimental to her marriage to acquiesce to her husband's wish to lie to the children about a particular family secret.

Another example I commonly encounter are wives who tolerate their husband's absence from family events even when they value family involvement. For husbands, a common problem is refusing to stand up to their wives when their wives become dominant and controlling, even though the husband has the conviction that he should be the leader of the family. These are not acts of kindness but rather actions emanating from unaddressed issues regarding fear and passivity. The Bible rejects passivity as a means of kindness. Instead, we are encouraged to, "Stand firm and hold to the teachings passed on to us." (2 Thessalonians 2:15)

Enabling Inappropriate Behavior

Rescuing one's spouse from the natural consequences of their irresponsible or foolish behavior is not an act of kindness. Nevertheless, rescuing continues to be a common problem in many unhappy marriages. Sometimes husbands or wives are so determined to protect their spouses from painful consequences, they unwittingly reinforce destructive behavior.

A common example of this type of rescuing is the spouse who makes excuses and rationalizes the angry outbursts and exasperating actions of his or her spouse. Proverbs speaks clearly to this issue: "A hot-tempered man must pay the penalty; if you rescue him, you will have to do it again." (Proverbs 19:19) Spouses who rescue eventually face the same situation again and again until the rescuing ceases. Rescuing may seem kind in the sense that the hurtful spouse feels less pain in the moment; however, in the long run, they continue to experience guilt and shame regarding their actions and sadly lose respect for their partner for tolerating unacceptable behavior.

Empty Words

Husbands and wives do not enjoy seeing their partner suffer from a heavy heart. Therefore, it is natural for them to want to reduce the discomfort of their spouse. Unfortunately, the means by which they attempt to do this often exacerbates their spouse's sadness rather than alleviating it. This is certainly the case when spouses employ the tactic of speaking light words of cheer. Proverbs affirms the futility of this approach: "Like one who takes away a garment on a cold day, or like vinegar poured on soda, is one who sings songs to a heavy heart." (Proverbs 25:20) Phrases such as, "Don't worry," "Cheer up," "Look at the bright side" or "Count your blessings," typically are not comforting or soothing when a spouse is feeling down. This is because they are not really kind responses at all, but rather self-serving responses designed to reduce one's own discomfort with pain and helplessness.

Quick Advice

The final type of false kindness is quick advice. The epistle of James advises Christians to be quick to listen and slow to speak (James 1:19). Proverbs states, "A man of knowledge uses words with restraint, and a man of understanding is even-tempered. Even a fool is thought wise if he keeps silent, and discerning if he holds his tongue." (Proverbs 17:27-28)

In my private practice, I ask couples to refrain from advice and problem solving until they fully understand the problem from the perspective of their spouses and have communicated that understanding to their spouses. I find that husbands and wives generally feel more connected when empathy and validation either precede advice giving, or in some cases, replace it altogether. Typically, husbands struggle with the temptation to problem solve the most. However, wives with stronger personalities also find it difficult to resist advice giving. I teach this principle to my clients by telling them that it is better to solve the relationship with empathy and understanding than to solve the problem with advice.

Questions for Reflection:

1. Share with your partner a time when you experienced them as being kind.

2. In what ways would you enjoy experiencing kindness from your partner?

3. What acts of "False Kindness" are you susceptible to?

Weekly Challenge:

First of all, do something kind for your partner this week. At the end of the week, see if they can guess what you did. Secondly, pick a day this week and count your acts of kindness for that day. How did counting your acts of kindness affect your mood and attitude?

~ Chapter 11 ~

Peace

"Blessed are the peacemakers for they will be called sons of God." (Matthew 5:9)

"Love your neighbor as you love yourself. If you go on hurting each other and tearing each other apart, be careful, or you will completely destroy each other." (Galatians 5:14-15)

"Make every effort to keep the unity of the Spirit through the bond of peace." (Ephesians 4:3)

Peacemaking refers to the action of resolving marital conflict through the application of understanding, vulnerability, humility, confession and insight. One truth I often point out to couples is that the Bible says blessed are the "peacemakers" not blessed are the "peace keepers." The wording is appropriate because conflict is inevitable in any healthy human relationship, including marriage. Therefore, our goal ought not to be to avoid conflict in order to keep peace but rather to resolve conflict in order to make peace.

Research confirms the positive correlation between conflict resolution and marital satisfaction (Schneewind & Gerhard, 2002). Furthermore, conflict resolution skills and good communication have been found to protect couples from marital divorce and dissatisfaction (Freedman, Low, Markman & Stanley, 2002).

Contrary to what most couples might think, the expression of complaints is not necessarily destructive to marriage. Psychologist John Gottman offers a helpful distinction between complaints which are healthy and criticisms which are destructive (Gottman, 1994). According to Gottman, complaints are positive and specific statements of concern that lead to the resolution of conflict. An example of a healthy complaint might be, "We haven't gone out to a movie in over a month. I'd like to go to a movie this weekend." In contrast, a criticism is a statement that belittles, demeans or shames a person in order to get them to behave the way you would like. An example of a criticism is, "You never take me to the movies anymore. All you care about when you come home is watching television or playing on the computer. You are so selfish." It comes as no surprise that research has found that criticisms are one of the leading contributors to the escalation of conflict and the erosion of marital satisfaction (Gottman, 1994).

Some of you reading this chapter may be wondering, "Doesn't the Bible exhort us to not complain or argue with one another?" In fact, there is a passage in Philippians which is translated in the New International Version of the Bible: "Do everything without complaining or arguing, so that you may become blameless and pure, children of God" (Philippians 2:14a) The interesting thing about this passage, however, is that the Greek word for complaining means to express displeasure or to grumble in a manner which promotes ill will instead of harmony. This sounds more like criticism than a healthy complaint. As Christians, we are free to express our disappointments as long as we do so in a manner that promotes good will and eventually leads to harmony.

In my private practice, I teach couples three main aspects of conflict resolution: Mutual Understanding, Solution Finding and Evaluation.

Mutual Understanding

In the Mutual Understanding phase couples first set a time and a place for the discussion of the conflict or problem. The goal is to talk together calmly without distractions or time constraints. This is especially important for couples with children. A Saturday morning visit to the local coffee shop is great example of an appropriate time and place.

The discussion starts when either the husband or wife begins to share his or her perspective on the problem or conflict. His or her spouse listens carefully and attentively. While listening to one another, it is important to edit out all distractions, especially defensive responses and counter complaints. The listener will have ample opportunity to share their thoughts and feelings when the roles are reversed. You should only switch roles when the speaker is completely confident that the listener understands the issue from the speaker's perspective. During this stage it is helpful for the listener to ask the question, "Is there anything else you would like to say?" before switching roles. It may also be helpful for the listener to paraphrase back to the speaker a concise and coherent summary of what was said. A helpful tool for reflecting back what you hear is to start your statement with a phrase such as, "What I hear you saying is..." or "It sounds like you are saying...."

A helpful tip for the listeners is to validate what they are hearing after they have communicated understanding. It is important to remember that validating a perspective is not the same as agreeing with it. Validation simply means that you can understand the speaker's point of view. I recommend the following statements to communicate validation:

"That makes sense to me"

"I see your point."

"I can understand how you see it that way."

Another helpful tip for the listener is to communicate comfort and reassurance whenever the opportunity arises. For instance, if a wife is fearful that her husband no longer finds her attractive, he can reassure her that he still thinks she is beautiful. Or, if a husband is afraid of losing his job, his wife can provide comfort by reminding him that she is willing to go back to work if necessary.

For the speaker, it is important to share what is happening from his or her perspective, what it means, how he or she feels about it and what he or she desires. I recommend that couples do this by using what psychologists refer to as "I" statements. Throughout the marital communication literature many different formats for "I" statements are recommended. Below is a rubric I use with my couples:

When you _____

I get the impression _____

And I feel _____

And I would like _____

This format has several advantages. First of all, it differentiates between one's interpretation of what an action or behavior means and what actually happened. For instance, when a husband stays out late with his work colleagues, there are different possibilities of what this could mean to his wife. One wife might get the impression that her husband is selfish. Another might have the impression that her husband is disinterested in her and still another might interpret the action as payback for her insistence that he start coming home from work earlier. In other words, the interpretation of what a particular behavior means to a particular spouse is idiosyncratic and contextual. This is important because our affective response to one another is directly related to our interpretation of what a behavior means as opposed to the actual behavior itself.

A second advantage of this technique is that it forces couples to find and express the feelings that are evoked by a particular interpretation of a behavior. Generally, when feelings are expressed, one's partner becomes less defensive and more cooperative. If possible, it is best to articulate what psychologists call "primary feelings" rather than "secondary feelings." This is helpful because the expression of a primary feeling usually involves more transparency, authenticity and vulnerability, all of which are disarming in a conflict discussion. A common example of a secondary feeling I see in my private practice is anger. When I hear a spouse say they are feeling angry, I ask them what primary feelings are underneath the anger. If they can't come up with anything, I will offer some suggestions. Often times we can find feelings such as hurt, shame, embarrassment, insignificance and fear. Discovering these feelings usually opens the door for new patterns of interaction and increases feelings of attachment and intimacy.

In order to find a primary feeling, many couples find it helpful to choose from a list of potential feelings. Here is an example of a list I use with couples:

> Afraid, embarrassed, desperate, anxious, overwhelmed, insecure

> Sad, alone, forgotten, pushed out, ignored, attacked,

Devalued, unimportant, worthless, unloved, belittled, betrayed

Pressured, panicked, shocked, surprised

Helpless, powerless, hopeless, empty, abandoned,

Ashamed, guilty

The final advantage to this approach is that it allows couples to ask for what they want. Jesus said, "For everyone who asks receives...." (Matthew 7:8a) I encourage couples to ask for a specific behavioral change. For example instead of asking, "Can you be more involved in our son's life?" I would encourage a spouse to ask, "Can you start taking Bradley to his baseball practices." A good rule of thumb for differentiating between a general request and a specific request is to ask, "Is the behavior I am asking for something that can be clearly identified by an independent observer looking at a videotape?"

The next step in the Mutual Understanding phase involves both spouses humbly and honestly acknowledging their contribution to the conflict or problem. A good question to ask is, "Is there some truth to my spouse's complaint about my behavior?" This is the time to apologize for transgressions, admit mistakes and acknowledge shortcomings. This is easier to do when we remind ourselves that God knows we are all imperfect and fall short of His original design. It is also easier to practice humility when we remind ourselves that God's love and value for us is not contingent upon our performance and that He often works best in us when we surrender to Him. In fact, the Bible says that God "Gives grace to the humble and guides them in what is right." (Psalm 25:9)

Humility has the power to disarm our spouses when they are angry and upset. Humility creates a safe environment where honest self-disclosure can continue uninhibited and mutual understanding and compassion flourish. For instance, if Sherry is upset that her husband Steve has embarrassed his son by disciplining him in a public place, Steve could humbly respond by saying, "You're right honey, I know I tend to do that, and I'm sorry. I will apologize to our son when I see him tonight." Sherry will likely calm down, forgive Steve and gently ask that in the future Steve discipline their son in private.

On the other hand, if Steve responds with pride and arrogance, the conflict will likely escalate. Suppose Steve says, "If Luke would stop antagonizing his sister, then I wouldn't have to correct him. He's not embarrassed. He's just manipulating you again." In this case Sherry will likely feel dismissed, attacked and criticized and may counter with something like this. " I'm sorry we can't all be perfect like you." Now the couple is headed for either a heated fight or a lengthy and cold silence.

A final recommendation for couples throughout the Mutual Understanding phase is to carefully think through the meaning of the conflict or problem in light of past relationships, especially family of origin relationships. A good question to ask is, "How is this current relational interaction an approximate replay of relational interactions from my past?" Another good question is, "When have I felt this way before, and what happened to me then that I am afraid is going to happen now?"

Case Study: Jay And Stacy

>As an example, suppose Jay feels frustrated when his wife Stacy continually interrupts him before he finishes sharing his thoughts and feelings about their financial difficulties. Each time Stacy interrupts, Jay feels annoyed, ignored and devalued. He eventually gives up trying to communicate and retreats into an icy silence. In this example, the intensity of Jay's negative feelings is exacerbated by the resemblance between the current interaction and the interactions he had with his mother. When Jay was a child, he vividly remembers being unable to fully convey his thoughts and feelings to his mother because of her frequent interruptions. Furthermore, when Jay asked his Mother to let him finish speaking, she would fall apart and cry. Jay would then feel guilty and ashamed for hurting her feelings. He would react to these feelings by retreating to his bedroom and listening to music for solace.

>Jay's family of origin experiences not only affect the intensity of his emotional response, but also his style of interacting with his wife. For instance, Jay does not ask Stacy to let him finish speaking because he is

afraid she will be crushed like his mother. In addition, he withdraws from Stacy as soon as he begins to feel devalued believing that it is hopeless to change things in the present just as it was hopeless to change things in the past.

Unfortunately, Jay doesn't know that his spouse may be similar to his mother but not an exact replica of her. This is often the case in the marriages I see. I teach couples that styles of responding to distressing feelings that were adaptive in the "then and there" of their lives may be maladaptive in the "here and now" of their lives. In this specific example, Jay may discover that his mother interrupted him because of her own anxiety about his disclosures and unconsciously chose to devalue and dismiss Jay rather than experience what felt like intolerable anxiety.

On the other hand, Stacy may interrupt Jay because in her family of origin, interrupting was interpreted as a sign of interest whereas silence was interpreted as disinterest. Therefore, if Jay learns this truth about Stacy, he can be freed up to ask Stacy to convey her interest in a different manner by letting him finish before she speaks. Stacy will likely comply because she is actually interested in what Jay has to say, and Jay will in turn feel valued, important and attended to.

The above example also illustrates the need for each spouse to ask two more important questions during the Mutual

Understanding phase. The first question is, "What evidence do I have that my spouse is the same as my parent? The second question is, "What evidence do I have that my spouse is different?" The similarities may lead to the triggering or exacerbation of feelings or the implementation of an old interactional strategy that is no longer useful. The differences allow for risk taking and the employment of new interactional styles that lead to better outcomes than one has experienced in the past. Finally, this example shows how insightful discussion of a conflict or problem can lead to new healing for old family of origin injuries.

Insights into one's family of origin can also be useful to spouses who are trying to understand and convey the important symbolic meaning underlying a particular issue.

Case Study: Larry And Lisa

> For example, Larry and his wife Lisa are looking for ways to decrease their spending in order to balance their budget. Lisa suggests that Larry not renew his hockey season tickets for the following year. Larry responds with indignation and distress that surprises his wife. Fortunately, Lisa responds by gently asking Larry why he feels so strongly about keeping the tickets rather than criticizing him for being inflexible and selfish. Larry is also surprised by the intensity of his reaction to Lisa's suggestion and wonders how this issue might be triggering something from his childhood. He remembers as a child being passionate about playing

hockey and watching his favorite team on television. He also remembers dreaming of attending a game at the local arena with his father. Sadly, he also remembers his father scolding him for having the nerve to ask for tickets they couldn't afford. Larry vowed to himself as a child that he would someday be able to take his son to hockey games. As Larry looked deeper into this, he realized that the season tickets not only represented his desire to pursue his passions in life but also to have a father/son connection he missed out on with his detached and depressed father.

After Larry shared this with Lisa she suggested they find another way to cut their costs. What is interesting to note is that at this point, Larry offered to sell tickets to games he would not be able to attend with his son once he realized the true meaning that the tickets held for him.

Solution Finding

The second phase of the conflict resolution process requires couples to come up with potential solutions to problems or conflicts that they are willing to try out. In this phase, couples discover the true needs underlying the stated requests. After this has been achieved, the couple then brainstorms potential solutions freely and without interruption, questioning or debate. Finally, the couple selects one or two solutions to implement.

For example, Mary suggests to Frank that they go out this Saturday night for a romantic dinner. Frank responds abruptly, "We can't afford to go out to dinner, and I hate having to pay so much for babysitting." In response to Frank's comment, Mary feels not only dejected but rejected as well. She retreats to her room to read her latest romance novel where she can at least vicariously experience the romance she so desperately misses in her own marriage.

In this example what Mary really wants is not a fancy dinner out but rather a romantic experience with her husband. What Frank really wants is to be a good steward of the resources God has given him, not to turn down his wife's invitation. If they are able to understand this, they are more likely to come up with a solution that meets both of their needs. For instance, they can offer to do a babysitting exchange with a neighbor rather than pay for a sitter. They can pack a dinner and take it down to the beach where Frank first proposed to Mary. This way they each get what they want: romance at an affordable price.

Case Study: Tom And Jill

> In another example, Tom tells his wife Jill that he would like to coach their 6-year-old son Jake in the upcoming fall baseball season. Jill feels anxious and asks Tom to wait until the spring season because she wants Jake to only play one sport at a time. Jill reminds Tom that Jake has already chosen to play soccer this fall. At this point, Tom can either accuse Jill of being unreasonable

or he can collaborate with her to find a creative win/win solution.

After some discussion, it becomes clear to Tom that Jill isn't necessarily against Jake playing baseball, but rather is concerned about being overwhelmed with parenting demands such as watching the children, doing laundry and driving the kids to their activities. In addition, Jill realizes that Tom has a dream of coaching Jake that is directly related to Tom's own childhood experience. Tom became tearful as he described to Jill how disinterested his own father was in Tom's baseball career which nearly took Tom to the major leagues.

During the initial brainstorming session, Tom suggests that he drive Jake to his baseball practices and games. Jill suggests that Jake quit soccer. After they finish brainstorming, they realize that neither of these suggestions would work. Jill reminds Tom, that even with Tom driving Jake to practices and games, she would still have the added task of cleaning stained uniforms. Tom reminds Jill that Jake wants to play soccer to be with his friends, and Tom doesn't want Jake to feel alienated from his friends.

At an impasse, yet armed with new knowledge, the couple agrees to brainstorm for a second time. This time Tom suggests that he take Jake's baseball uniforms to the cleaners along with his dirty work clothes so that Jill will have even less laundry than before. Furthermore,

Tom suggests that he bring his 4-year-old son Justin along to practices to give Jill some time to herself. Jill agrees because she gets what she really needs, which is a less demanding life, and Tom agrees because he gets what he really needs, which is to coach his son in baseball and allow his son to enjoy playing sports with his friends.

Evaluation

The final phase of the peacemaking process is evaluation. In this phase, the couple examines whether the solutions they chose to implement are actually working. In the last example, Tom asks Jill midway through the fall baseball season if she is feeling that her life is manageable. Jill checks in with Tom to see how well he is balancing work with his new demands as a baseball coach. She also checks in to see if having Jake's younger brother Justin at the practices has presented a problem for Tom. If things are going well they can count their solution as a success. If there are problems, they can go back to phase one and go back through the conflict resolution process again.

Questions for Reflection:

1. What is your typical response to conflict? Do you fight, retreat, ignore or yield?

2. What makes it difficult for you to engage in constructive conflict resolution with your partner?

3. Which aspect of the conflict resolution process will present the biggest challenge for you?

Weekly Challenge:

Pick a mild issue of disagreement between you and your partner. See if you can work through the conflict resolution process together and get to a win/win solution.

~ Chapter 12 ~

Maturity

"Then we will no longer be infants tossed back and forth by the waves, and blown here and there by every wind of teaching and by the cunning and craftiness of men in their deceitful scheming. Instead, speaking the truth in love, we will in all things grow up into him who is the Head, that is, Christ." (Ephesians 4:14-15)

"When I was a child, I talked like a child, I thought like a child, I reasoned like a child. When I became a man, I put childish ways behind me." (1 Corinthians 13:11)

Maturity in the context of marriage refers to the psychological and spiritual development of each spouse. It reflects the extent to which spouses are able to act with an age appropriate degree of autonomy while also accepting responsibility for their decisions and behaviors. Psychological research has shown that maturity is highly associated with overall marital adjustment (Quinn, 1998). Furthermore, "differentiation," a concept closely related to emotional maturity, has also been found to positively correlate with marital satisfaction (Kosek, 1998; Skowron, 2000).

Spiritual maturity and psychological maturity are reciprocally and positively correlated. One cannot exist without the other, and each enhances the growth of the other. Together they promote a strong and healthy marital bond. There are three important components to maturity: (1) Putting away childish behaviors, (2) Giving up old habits and (3) Developing growth-promoting character traits.

Putting Away Childish Behavior

First, each spouse needs to put away childish behaviors. The apostle Paul puts it this way, "When I was a child, I talked like a child, I thought like a child, I reasoned like a child. When I became a man, I put childish ways behind me." (1 Corinthians 13:11)

Below is a list of childish behaviors that can lead to trouble in marriage:

    Selfishness
    Tantrums
    Pouting
    Demanding immediate gratification
    Low frustration tolerance
    Emotional reasoning
    Making excuses
    Inflexibility

Dishonesty
Conditional love
Avoiding confrontation

Perhaps you can relate to some of the items on the above list. If so, discuss them with your spouse and make a commitment to consciously and intentionally remove these childish reactions from your marriage. Ask the Holy Spirit to give you the power to say no to the impulse to respond in childish ways. Finally, practice more mature ways of relating and behaving.

Giving Up Old Habits

The second component of maturity is to give up habitual ways of relating to your spouse that were once adaptive in the past but are maladaptive in the current marriage. Doing this is easier said than done for two reasons. First of all, there is a false belief deep in one's heart that the best approach to future relationships is always what has worked in the past. This is sometimes but not always true. Furthermore, it is less true when a spouse has been raised in a family system where healthy behavior was discouraged.

For example, Tim grew up in a family where verbal expressions of affirmation were eschewed in the name of promoting humility. Now Tim is married to Lily, and one of Lily's main complaints is that Tim doesn't affirm her enough and cannot take a compliment without being self-dismissive. Tim's approach to verbal affirmation worked well in his family of origin but does not work well with his wife. Lily's family promoted verbal praise and viewed such praise as an expression of love. Tim has inferred from his experience that verbal affirmations promote pride and are not a means of expressing love. However, if Tim is going to love Lily in a way that feels loving to her, he is going to have see things differently. Below is a list of other behaviors that are often adaptive in dysfunctional family systems and maladaptive in a healthy marriage.

- Compulsively performing to be noticed and accepted by others
- Yelling to get someone to listen
- Being self-sufficient to get your needs met
- Being more logical to avoid being shamed for your feelings
- Downplaying your successes to make others feel more worthwhile
- Giving the silent treatment to let someone know you are hurt and upset
- Acting strong when you feel weak, so as not to be shamed and humiliated
- Holding back words of affirmation and affection so as not to embarrass others
- Retreating into fantasy when reality is too painful
- Accommodating to the wishes of others rather than asserting your own desires
- Getting quiet when conflict arises
- Solving the problems of others

If you find yourself falling into this trap of falling into old maladaptive modes of relating, it is important not to beat yourself up. Remind yourself that you did what was best for your survival and protection as a child. It's just no longer necessary to function in that manner. It is likely that you have married a safer person who is more tolerant and accepting of healthy ways of relating. Therefore, it is probably going to be good for your marriage to take risks with new behaviors especially when old behaviors seem to be damaging to your relationship.

Developing Growth-Promoting Character Traits

The third component of maturity is to acquire and develop growth-promoting character traits. An exhaustive listing of such traits could be the topic of an entire book. For our purposes, I have identified six growth-promoting traits that are supported by Scripture.

Perseverance

James makes a clear connection between perseverance and maturity when he writes, "Perseverance must finish its work so that you may be mature and complete, not lacking anything." (James 1:4) Spouses who persevere continue to love even when they receive nothing in return. They are not deterred by adverse circumstances and undesirable outcomes. They know what God wants them to do, and they do it out of love for Him not in order to attain some positive outcome.

They have faith that ultimately things will work together for good (Romans 8:28) even when in the midst of current trials and tribulations.

The apostle Paul demonstrated perseverance in his continuing efforts to preach the Gospel despite continual derision, ridicule and opposition from those he was trying to reach. Paul pressed onward because he saw it as the mature thing to do. In his letter to the Philippians he wrote about this: "I press on toward the goal to win the prize for which God has called me heavenward in Christ Jesus. All of us who are mature should take such a view of things. And if on some point you think differently that too God will make clear to you." (Philippians 3:15)

A second aspect of perseverance involves refusing to quit when you are not behaving as you wish. I have observed in my private counseling that the most meaningful actions are often the hardest to do. They are not impossible however. With enough practice, what once seemed difficult can become natural and automatic. I recall a client who felt unimportant and devalued by her husband because he rarely asked her for help. Gradually, with practice and his wife's patience, her husband slowly began to articulate his needs and allowed her to help. The effect of this change was positive for both wife and husband.

Accepting Feedback

In the book of Proverbs we read, "As iron sharpens iron, so

one man sharpens another." (Proverbs 27:17) In marriage, husbands and wives have the potential to either sharpen each other or alienate each other with feedback. It all depends on how the feedback is given and how it is received. A great way to give constructive feedback is to use the "sandwich" technique. Start by affirming your spouse, then give your constructive feedback and end with another affirmation. This will make it easier for your spouse to digest and metabolize the feedback they received and hopefully use it for their own growth.

The listener needs to receive feedback non-defensively. Ask yourself, "Is there some truth to what my spouse is saying?" Also, remember that God can speak truth to you through an imperfect human being. Therefore, it is important not to fall into a defensive posture such as counter-attacking, making excuses or blaming others. It is best to remind ourselves that God is not done with any of us and simply accept responsibility where needed and commit to make a change for the better.

Initiative

Initiative refers to the anticipation of your spouse's needs and proactive behavior that addresses these needs. Simply stated, it is "doing what needs to be done without having to be asked." Spouses who initiate reject passivity. They behave like the ant described in Proverbs: "Go to the ant, you sluggard, consider its ways and be wise! It has no commander, no overseer or ruler yet it stores its provisions in summer and gathers its food at harvest." (Proverbs 6:6) The ant thinks ahead. The ant does what is necessary without being asked. The ant is considered wise. And lastly, we are wise to consider its ways.

A second aspect of initiative involves continually working to create a climate conducive to positive behavioral change in your spouse rather than feeling helpless and hopeless when desired changes are not occurring. For example, suppose Jack is feeling discouraged because his wife Carla continues to say she is too tired for intimacy at the end of the day. Instead of lamenting his poor choice of a sexual partner, Jack can work at creating a climate which contributes to Carla being less tired and more sexually interested in Jack in the evenings. This can include a variety of things such as helping out more with the children and the household chores, taking Carla out on romantic dates, complementing Carla on her appearance and possibly even hiring a housekeeper.

Self-Control

The Bible warns us in Proverbs 25:28, "Like a city where walls are broken down is a man who lacks self-control." Proverbs 12:18 adds, "Reckless words pierce like a sword." It is commonly stated that it is healthy to control one's emotions. I disagree. Emotions are not the problem. The problem is how we respond to our emotions, especially intense emotions. The apostle Paul says, "In your anger do not sin." (Ephesians 4:24) The issue for couples is how to respond in healthy ways when anger, frustration, pain and fear are flooding their hearts. Husbands and wives with self-control do not respond automatically and impulsively. Rather, they stop, pay attention to their feelings, think about a proper response and then execute that response. This is not easy, but it is an extremely helpful. Self-control is like a muscle. If you exercise it, then it will grow stronger. If you don't, it will atrophy, and you will find many more instances of escalated conflict and fighting in your marriage.

The Bible identifies self-control as one of the fruits of the Spirit (Ephesians 5:22). As we mature in our faith, we will also see greater evidence of self-control in our lives. Thus, we are not alone in our quest to master self-control. The Holy Spirit helps us and works through us to produce this fruit.

Standing Firm

Standing firm refers to the act of holding fast to a conviction despite resistance from one's spouse. For example, Spencer explains to his wife Joan that they can save money on taxes by failing to claim the cash money he earned in his construction business this year. Joan believes this is not only unethical but also goes against the command of Jesus who admonished his followers to, "Give to Caesar what was due to Caesar." (Matthew 22:21) Spencer teases Joan saying that she knows nothing about the realities of the business world and should stop sticking her nose in his business. He then adds that they can use the extra money for the children's educational expenses. In this situation, Joan would do well to hold her ground and request that they pay taxes on every dollar they earned during the year. This choice aligns her with the Paul who has encouraged us to "Stand firm in all the will of God, mature and fully assured." (Colossians 4:12)

Joan's stance helps her marriage in two ways. First of all, it will prohibit a buildup of resentment and disrespect in Joan's heart which will inevitably result in a loss of intimacy between her and her husband. Secondly, Joan's decision may motivate Spencer to reexamine the discrepancies in his life between what he preaches and what he practices.

Self-Awareness

The writer of Proverbs teaches us that, "The purposes of a man's heart are deep waters but a man of understanding draws them out." (Proverbs 20:5) There are several ways spouses can develop an increased understanding of why they do what they do. People can learn about themselves through self-observation, feedback from others, introspection and quietly listening to the voice of God. However, one of the best ways to develop self-awareness is through professional counseling. Many people are averse to this option because they assume that only "crazy" people are in psychotherapy. I disagree. Psychotherapy with a competent Christian counselor can be one of the richest and most rewarding experiences for anyone interested in growth and development. A wise counselor can help us understand the reasons both conscious and unconscious behind our thoughts, feelings and behavior. In terms of marriage, a well-trained counselor can teach spouses how to relate to each other in more loving, productive and healthy ways.

Case Study: Rachel And Greg

Here is an example of the benefits of self-awareness for marriage. Rachel has a long-standing history of refusing to forgive her husband Greg for his various transgressions over the years. In her individual counseling, she recounts how unforgiving her mother was toward her father. The counselor points out to Rachel that she has identified with her own mother by relating to her husband the same way her mother related to her father.

Rachel begins to understand her behavior as an unconscious attempt to protect her mother. Rachel discovers that when she unconsciously perpetuates the intergenerational family legacy of unforgiveness, she is normalizing her mother's behavior. Rachel further understands that her desire to protect her mother in this manner is fueled by her need for secure relational connection with her mother.

This hypothesis is confirmed when Rachel recalls instances of feeling shunned by her mother for being "too forgiving" of her father. Rachel clearly remembers a specific time when her father, who rarely missed her basketball games had to work overtime, and therefore missed one of her last games of the season. Rachel remembers being scolded by her mother for forgiving her father. The recounting of these experiences in the safety of her counselor's office, and the insights regarding the connections between past and present behavior will likely free Rachel up to respond to her husband in more forgiving ways in the future.

Questions for Reflection:

1. What are some old habits you need to break? How were they adaptive in your childhood? How are they maladaptive now?

2. What growth-promoting trait do you want to develop? How will you do this?

3. What are your thoughts seeking out personal counseling? Share these with your partner.

Weekly Challenge:

Experiment with a new way of relating to your partner this week that is different than the way you related to your parents. Discuss with your partner how it felt and how well it seemed to work.

References

Blodgett, P. (1997). Six ways to be a better listener. *Training & Development, 51*(7), 11-12.

Cunningham, B. (2001). The will to forgive: A pastoral theological view of forgiving. *Journal of Pastoral Care, 39*(2), 141-150.

Curry, O. (2008). Patience is a virtue: Cooperative people have lower discount rates. *Personality and Individual Differences, 44*(3), 780-785.

Davis, M.H., & Oathout, H.A. (1987). Maintenance of satisfaction in romantic relationships: empathy and relational competence. *Journal of Personality and Social Psychology, 53*, 397-410.

Emmons, R. (2000). Personality and forgiveness. In M.E. McCullough, K.I. Pargament, & C.E. Thoresen (Eds.), Forgiveness: Theory, research, and practice (pp.156-175). New York: Guilford.

Emmons, R. (2007). Patience as a virtue: Religious and psychological perspectives. *Research in the Social Scientific Study of Religion, 18*, 177-207.

Fee, G. (1987). The First Epistle to the Corinthians, in The New International Commentary on the New Testament, edited by F.F. Bruce, Grand Rapids, Eerdmans Publishing, p. 638.

Freedman, C., Low, S., Markman, H., &Stanley, S. (2002). Equipping couples with the tools to cope with predictable and unpredictable crisis events: The Prep Program. *International Journal of Emergency Mental Health, 4*(1), 49-56.

Gaebler, M. (2002). Luther on the self. *Journal of the Society of Christian Ethics, 22*, 126.

Gottman, J. (1994). Why marriages succeed or fail. New York. Simon & Schuster.

Hooda, D. (2009). Social intelligence as a predictor of positive psychological health. *Journal of the Indian Academy of Applied Psychology, 35*(1), 143-150.

Knox, D., Schacht, C., Holt, J., & Turner, J. (1993). Sexual lies among university students. *College Student Journal, 27*, 269-272.

Kosek, R. B. (1998). Self-differentiation within couples. *Psychological Reports, 83*, 275-279.

Lauer, R.H., Lauer, J.C., & Kerr, S.T. (1990). The long-term marriage: perceptions of stability and satisfaction. *International Journal of Aging and Human Development, 31*, 189-195.

Leifer, R. (1996). Psychological and spiritual factors in chronic illness. *American Behavioral Scientist, 39*(6), 752-766.

Levine, T., & McCornack, S. (1992). Linking love and lies: A formal test of the McCornack and Parks model of deception detection. *Journal of Social and Personal Relationships, 9*, 143-154.

McCornack, S. & Levine, T. (1990). When lies are uncovered: Emotional and relational outcomes of discovered deception. Communication Monographs, 57, 119-138.

Miller, T., Smith, T., Turner, C., Guijarro, M. & Hallet, A. (1996). A meta-analytic review of research on hostility and physical health. *Psychological Bulletin, 119*, 322-348.

Otake, K. (2006). Happy people become happier through kindness: A counting kindness intervention. *Journal of Happiness Studies, 7*(3), 361-375.

Peck, S. (1978). The road less traveled. New York, Simon and Schuster.

Quinn, W. (1998). Predictors of marital adjustment during the first two years. *Marriage and Family Review, 27*(1-2), 113-130.

Rimland, B. (1982). The altruism paradox. *Psychological Reports, 51*(2), 521-522.

Rowan, D.G., Compton, W.C. & Rust, J.O. (1995). Self-actualization and empathy as predictors of marital satisfaction. *Psychological Reports, 77*, 1011-1016.

Sappington, A. (1998). Wrath: Relationships between sinful anger, blaming cognitions, and altruism. *Journal of Psychology and Christianity, 17* (1), 25-32.

Schneewind, K., & Gerhard, A. (2002). Relationship personality, conflict resolution, and marital satisfaction in the first 5 years of marriage. *Family Relations, 51*(1), 63-72.

Seybold, K., Hill, P., Neumann, J., & Chi, D. (2001). Physiological and psychological correlates of forgiveness. *Journal of Psychology and Christianity, 20*, (3), 250-259.

Skowron, E. A. (2000). The role of differentiation of self in marital adjustment. *Journal of Counseling Psychology, 47*, 229-237.

Smedes, L. (1978). Love within limits. Grand Rapids, Eerdmans.

Smedes, L. (2001). Keys to forgiving: how do you know that you have truly forgiven someone? *Christianity Today, 45*, 73-76.

Stanley, S., Trathen, D., McCain, S. & Bryan, M. (1998). *A lasting promise: A Christian guide to fighting for your marriage.* San Francisco: Jossey-Bass.

Stiff, J., Kim, H., & Ramesh, C. (1992). Truth biases and aroused suspicion in relational deception. *Communication Research, 19*, 326-345.

Tournier, P. (1967). To understand each other. Richmond, John Knox Press. In Wright, N. (1971). The living marriage. Old Tappan, NJ: Revell.

Waite, L., Browning, D., Doherty, W., Gallagher, M., Luo, Y., & Stanley, S., (2002). Does divorce make people happy? Findings from a study of unhappy marriages. Institute for American Values, NY, NY.

Waring, E., Schaefer, B., & Fry, R. (1994). The influence of therapeutic self-disclosure on perceived marital intimacy. *Journal of Sex & Marital Therapy. 20*(2) 135-146.

Worthington, E. (1993). Value your mate. Grand Rapids, Baker Books.

Acknowledgments

Thank you Janelle. You have taught me more about marriage than I could ever imagine. You are my soul-mate, my inspiration, and my best friend.

Thank you Chris and Stace, John and Orielle, Steve and Crestine and Alex and Sherry. Your prayers and support have been invaluable. May we continue to grow through life together.

Mahalo to my best friends Dean and Derek. I love you guys with all my heart.

Thanks to my mentors Dr. Kim Storm and Dr. Jon Peterson. Your collective wisdom never ceases to amaze me.

A special thanks to my Pastor and my friend Jeff Pries. You have believed in me from the start and given me so many wonderful opportunities to minister to young couples at Mariners Church. I am forever grateful.

Thank you to my parents who have modeled commitment and self-sacrifice for 50 plus years of marriage.

Finally, thanks to Rachel and the rest of the team at Newbookpublishing for helping transform a dream into a reality.

About The Author

Dr. Buddy Mendez is a Professor of Psychology at Concordia University, Irvine. He is also a Clinical Psychologist with a private practice in Newport Beach, California specializing in the integration of Christianity and psychology. He received his Ph.D. in Clinical Psychology and his M.A. in Theology from Fuller Theological Seminary. He has appeared as a guest on "Good Morning America" and is a regular guest on the "In Studio" radio program on station KFUO. Dr. Mendez speaks frequently at churches and retreats on various topics relating to marriage and family life. For more information, you can look up Dr. Mendez at his website: Drbuddymendez.com.

Need additional copies?

To order more copies of
Ready, Set, Married
contact CertaPublishing.com

- ❐ Order online at CertaPublishing.com/ReadySetMarried

- ❐ Call 855-77-CERTA or

- ❐ Email Info@CertaPublishing.com

Call for multiple copy discounts!